December 21st 2012

PREPARATION FOR YOUR TRANSFORMATION

G. Marshall Young

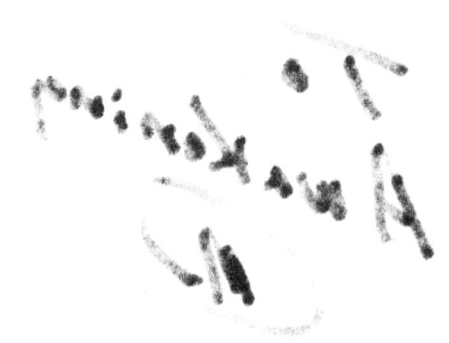

December 21^{st,} 2012
Preparation For Your Transformation

Wake Up Now Publications

Copyright © 2009 by G. Marshall Young

All rights reserved. No part of this book may be reproduced or transmitted in any form or by any means without written permission of the author.

ISBN 978-0-615-34393-8

ACKNOWLEDGMENT

"I once was lost but now I am found,
was blind but now I see..."

The book you are holding, <u>December 21, 2012 Preparation For Your Transformation,</u> has but one goal: to wake you up!

How addicted are you to your body, your mind, the earth and your programs? Have you ever thought about it? What if you knew that your addictions were keeping you in hell but there was a way out? Would you consider an escape from suffering or stay where you are?

You do not have a lot of time to answer the question. So, what do you want?

Coming from one who has struggled with addiction I can tell you that you are asleep but do not realize it. I can also tell you that there is a way out of this illusion if you are brave enough to take it. It will require a big change in perception.

The Planet Earth is not what you think it is and it is not your home.

There is a consciousness shift already underway. This book is a wake up call for those wanting out of the box. This book will help you see clearly, stop the redundancy of duality and give you the keys to conscious-awareness. You will need all of these to enter the new age.

You are holding in your hands a teaching tool, which will prepare you for a life-changing event. I have read many books, traveled to many places and have had a number of experiences that tell me we are entering a critical period in conscious evolution.

The books mentioned in the enclosed Bibliography helped stop my addictions, opened my eyes and saved my life. I have borrowed extensively from these sources to help you find the truth about who you are. I want to especially honor the following authors and highly recommend their books to assist you on your path to transformation:

Joseph Campbell, James Redfield, Kenneth Davis, Timothy Freke and Peter Gandy, Lloyd Graham, David Hawkins, Eckhart Tolle, Jon Mundy, A Course in Miracles and Conversations with Nisargaddata Maharaj – I AM THAT.

My understanding comes mainly from non-dimensional sources but the information by these authors will shorten your search. I can say from my experiences that enlightenment is better achieved through these references than anywhere else you could look. I have taught classes on all these references and believe that what I have chosen will clear up confusion, save you time and wake you up.

Don't take time for granted; you won't have that luxury forever.

I am in the process of creating a school to expand on the information and experiences outlined in this book. You may want to look into that after you read the book. Email me at wakeupnow2012@aol.com if you have further questions. You may also want to visit the web site www.wakeupnow201.com (currently under construction).

A new age is rapidly approaching and many historically famous Oracles, including the Mayan Calendar, are not missing the mark. Whether change is dramatic or subtle, change is inevitable. The reader needs to cut to the chase as time, as you have known it, is running out.

This book can only point the way. When you reach the end you will know what to do. An inner voice will tell you.

BIOGRAPHICAL SKETCH

Who Is This Guy Anyway?

Before I get into the information that could reveal a secret to you and change your life, let me tell you a little about my former life. It may help you understand who I am because of where I've been.

The information that follows is a brief biographical sketch starting with my arrival on this planet on October 14, 1941. I was born to a moderately successful but highly dysfunctional couple. As a young child I found love only in the arms of my grandmother, my aunts, uncles, cousins, dog and the Lutheran Church. I always feared my father and was not very close to my mother. My father passed away 35 years ago and my mother is still alive at age 92.

I attended my first four years of elementary school in a Lutheran church/school near Oklahoma City, Oklahoma. All of the classes were held in the basement of that church. Convinced I would someday become a pastor, I spent every waking minute away from home either at school, Sunday school, church services, Bible school or singing in the children's choir. Needless to say, the Church was my life and life away from home was good. On the other hand life at home was nightmarish with an alcoholic father and a distant mother. I didn't know it at the time but finding happiness away from home would become a pattern in my life. I hated home life.

Just as things seemed to be going okay, my father announced in 1950 that we would be moving to Waco, Texas because of his job. My life was shattered or so it seemed. We moved, I gave up my church activities and spent the next year walking the woods close to home with my dog. I hated school, hated my Dad and now I have a little brother who I didn't like very much either. Our family lasted only one year in Waco before we moved to a little South-Texas town called New Braunfels just north of San Antonio, Texas. Again because of my father's work.

New Braunfels was not all that bad. I learned to swim in the crystal clear Comal River, learned how to fish, spent a lot of time in the woods and stayed away from home as much as possible. My first rite of passage was making a little league baseball team. For the first time in my life I seemed to have an identity. School was a little better because of baseball, but my grades were not very good. Even though my mother was a schoolteacher, I cannot remember a single time where she helped me with my subjects and of course my father was never around or if he was he was either mad or drunk or both.

Junior High was another transition. The 7th and 8th grades were full of fights with Mexican kids, a failed attempt to play football, my first encounter with girls and a building anger inside me about my life in general. I was angry with the church, God, my parents, teachers and the older kids. It seemed liked I was getting my butt kicked by everyone.

My Dad surprised me three times in my life. He got me a black cocker spaniel puppy, Tony, when I was in the third grade, a set of golf clubs in the 5th grade and a horse in the 8th grade. The dog lived to be 22 and was a big part of my life. I figure the golf clubs were stolen and who knows where that horse came from, as my Dad was a city boy. I never played with the golf clubs until I was in the 9th grade because there was no golf course or anyone to teach me anything. The horse was another issue. I loved that old horse. She was 15 years old. I sometimes slept with her in a stable that I built from an old chicken coop in the back yard. She was my great escape. Sometimes I would let my brother ride her but she was my buddy and not to be shared with anyone. I looked forward to coming home from school, saddling up Frisky, who was anything but frisky, and be gone until dark. What freedom! It was a great time. But good times never lasted in our family.

My father was busted for possession of marijuana in 1954, my mom lost her teaching job and we were asked to leave the state. We sold the house and my horse, packed our furniture on a rental truck and headed north. I was 14 years old and with a one hour driving lesson from my angry father got behind the wheel of a truck and followed my parents out of the driveway to nowhere. I literally mean nowhere. In exchange for prosecution, the federal government allowed my Dad to resign his job without pension benefits or jail time and leave the state and never come back. We had no idea where we were headed. So, north it was.

As it turned out we wound up in Colorado and eventually in Colorado Springs. It was a five-day trip from Texas with all kinds of mechanical and weather problems. We had driven for five days and nights and by the fifth night reached a little cross roads town called Colorado Springs, Colorado. When I awoke on the morning of the sixth day and saw Pikes Peak, I was in shock! We all were. None of us had ever seen a mountain, not a real mountain. Having lived in Oklahoma and Texas you just couldn't imagine anything like a mountain. Well here we were and here we decided to stay. It's been my home off and on for nearly 55 years.

My second rite of passage came in 1955 when I enrolled as a freshman at Cheyenne Mountain High School in the south part of Colorado Springs. I became aware that football tryouts would begin in late August. So, I went out for football and was surprised to see there were no Mexican kids. What a relief. My Junior High School was nearly all Mexican kids and they just kicked our butts in every sport and after school on a regular basis.

I can't begin to explain how this all happened but there I was, a 130 pound (skinny) 14 year old kid with little to no experience playing football and getting my football equipment along side big 18 year old seniors. A bit scary. Everyone was pushing us freshmen around. Even the sophomores thought they were big stuff. While the first week of conditioning drills was hell the second week was where the second biggest thing in my life happened, to that point.

You need to understand that in those days there wasn't freshman or junior varsity football. There was only varsity meaning you either made the team or you turned in your equipment. It was on a hot August afternoon that it happened. Our coaches pulled us together and explained that we were going to find out who wanted to play and who would go home. The coaches separated the running backs in one group and the rest of us in another. Only two blocking dummies stood between the runners and the tacklers.

So, here's the deal. The running backs would get the football about 10 yards behind the two blocking dummies. They would run, full speed, between the dummies to be tackled, or run over by one downed lineman. Some of these backs were seniors at nearly 190 pounds. I am a soaking wet 130-pound freshman.

My side of tacklers was in a single line to take our turn on the field just like the running backs were in a single line to take their turn. The first two contacts were like watching a train wreck! The down tacklers never had a chance and were knocked backwards like bowling pins. I would be next in line and, as luck would have it, I would be facing the biggest senior full back on the team. I could hear everyone laughing behind me and some kid saying this is going to real funny.

And then it happened.

Like a movie in slow motion I said to myself, I will not be laughed at, I am not a quitter. I was tired of being left out of my life. I was angry with everyone and I would no longer be the fool even if I had to die that day on that spot. This was a new school, a new start and no one knew about my past.

I dropped to my knees and took a four-point stance. When the whistle blew I didn't wait, I attacked that kid and knocked him straight backwards fumbling the ball and losing his helmet. The only thing I remember hearing was the collision and my coach saying, "Now that's a real hit! Who was that man, get his name". Three more times that afternoon the same thing happened with the same results. I was dizzy, (almost unconscious) and bleeding from the nose and mouth. With tears in my eyes and determination in my heart, I sent four upper classmen to the dirt with the same reaction from my coaches and my teammates.

On that late summer afternoon I became a man. I knew it, my teammates knew it and my coaches knew it. I went on to start 44 consecutive games on both offense and defense, lettering all 4 years of high school. To my knowledge no one has ever duplicated or exceeded that accomplishment at Cheyenne Mountain High School before or since. No one ever called me out for a fight and everyone gave me respect, the first real respect I ever had. My coaches became my fathers and the football field became my field of dreams and it all happened in about 20 minutes on a hot day in August 1955.

It didn't happen because I was all that strong or experienced. It happened because I was fed up with being pushed around. It happened because my father was a mean drunk and beat up my mother. It happened because of a determination to succeed and never be ridiculed again. I was literally prepared to die rather than live in obscurity. It happened because God knew I would need that sense of power later on in life. It ranked as the most unbelievable day of my life up to having my spiritual revelations.

I played high school football, basketball, baseball and golf with the same determination but football was my game. I was a warrior in football and just did other sports to keep in shape. Because we had to have a 'C' average to play sports I kept my grades up to that level but it was a struggle. I was over my head most of the time in the classroom.

I had several girl friends, went to many a drinking party and was known as a rebel and a fighter. It was all that anger. I really had no close friends. I never did. I didn't respect anyone but my coaches and few other athletes. I stopped going to church completely by the 10th grade and thought most academic achievers were squares.

I went to Western State College In Gunnison, Colorado on a football scholarship in 1959 but it was not what I expected. I barely passed my classes and returned home after the first year. That summer I got my girl friend pregnant and married her in the fall. She was 18 and I was 19. What a mistake.

I hated what happened that summer. I hated it for her and her family and I hated myself for being so stupid.

I enrolled at Colorado University that Fall thinking I would play football for the Buffs but it wasn't to be. Those guys were too big, too fast and too smart. So, I walked out of school, getting all 'F's in five subjects, joined the Navy and went to California. The good news was that the U.S. Navy didn't think I was so hot and broke me down to be a good a sailor. This was another passage, another revelation.

My wife divorced me with good cause and returned to Colorado. I started doing a lot of drinking and some drugs just like my Dad who I hated for doing the same thing. Along came the Vietnam War and a new view on life. The war was a criminal enterprise and this country was filled with racial injustice. I became an active protestor of both.

I got another girl pregnant in 1962 and married her. I started back to school and worked nights for a rocket engine development company in the San Fernando Valley in So. California. I had to start from the beginning on my classes because all my grades were too bad to transfer. I did manage to graduate in 1967 with a B+ Average.

I was getting stoned on marijuana almost every day and drinking beer almost every night. I had a son and another baby on the way.

Following graduation and the Watts riots, in Los Angeles, which I participated in, and the assignation of Robert Kennedy who I worked for, I was just waiting around for the mass layoffs from the end of the aerospace program of the 1960's. For me it came in 1969.

My brother was in Vietnam as a marine killing machine. We both showed up in Colorado Springs about the same time after his discharge and my layoff. We both got stoned and drunk a lot together. He would tell me a little about the hell he went through in Vietnam and I started getting to know him better. I actually began to love my brother for the first time in my life. I never allowed myself to get close to him as kids. As it turned out he was a pretty nice guy. Imagine that?

I got a job teaching and coaching football in a little mountain town west of Colorado Springs. Now I had a son, a daughter, a hippie wife, a stoned brother, a runaway sister, a stoned, drunk father, a distant mother and was mostly broke. This was my life for the next three years until I started selling mountain land one summer in 1973. I made more money in my first six weeks of selling land than I did all year teaching and coaching seven days a week. Needless to say, I quit teaching and started selling mountain property but I still wasn't happy.

Something was missing in the middle of me but I didn't know what it was. I quit teaching school at $12,000 a year and got into real estate full time, making over $50,000 a year. What more could one ask for? As fate would have it I met another woman and wound up getting divorced for a second time and then remarried. Wife number three brought along five girls! How self-destructive was that?

After three years of selling land, two friends and myself created a real estate company with several salesmen and a life style that was pretty good. With the money came more expensive cars and drugs. I started using cocaine along with drinking and marijuana. I wound up getting my third divorce, selling my company and moving to Myrtle Beach, South Carolina in 1981. More money, more drugs and more women. This was my life for the next five years. Then on a trip home to Colorado Springs one Christmas my brother tells me he has given up drinking and drugs and has found "spiritual healing." I thought he had gone nuts or something and just couldn't believe it.

He asked me to go with him one night to hear a fellow named Mark give a talk. I admit I was amazed, but thought some spiritual snake oil salesman had taken my brother in. As it turned out my brother totally stopped drinking and drugging and became a member of the Summit Lighthouse. This was a very esoteric organization founded by Mark and Elizabeth Prophet. I was happy for him but no way ready to make that kind of commitment. So, I kept on doing my thing and occasionally talked to my brother about his new crazy life.

I was in physical and financial trouble by 1987 so I came back home to Colorado. I didn't work for three years. I met a nurse who told me about a program called Adult Children of Alcoholics (ACOA), which she thought I needed. As it turned out I needed it bad. I was in therapy for three years. The therapy trip got me in touch with my anger, fear and shame issues. I had no idea how angry I was and how hard I was trying to kill myself. For a while I cleaned up (stopped getting high) but fell off the wagon for a couple of years until I met my fourth (and final) wife.

Guess what, here comes the next revelation.

I was 50 years old, had been through several affairs, lots of drugs, gallons of booze, AA, therapy, my brother's revelation and still didn't get it.

Then it happened.

After a night of getting high I dreamed I was in a mortuary. Was it a dream? Yes, but it wasn't a mortuary. I was in a hospital on an Emergency Room bed having just suffered a cocaine-induced heart attack. In my dream state I was laying on a morgue table with my family and friends standing around. The mortician was saying how sad it was because I seemed to have so much potential. The mortician looked around the room and asked, "What shall we engrave on his tombstone?" It was like a scene from <u>A Christmas Carol</u>. Everyone looked at each other and then slowly at me and whispered "Looser"!

I came totally conscious and heard myself saying, "that's it, I'm not a looser or a quitter." My mind immediately shifted back to that hot August day in 1955 and my football experience. A blur of thoughts raced through my head. "Please give me another chance I cried. It's not my time, I can quit drugs and drinking, I will stop the lies. I don't want to die, not now!"

I can tell you it got my full attention. I went cold turkey on everything (spending over $1,000 a month on my addictions) and never gave it a second thought. I felt like I was being shown an opportunity for another chance and was thankful. In my dream state the decision to go straight or die had to be made right then. I obviously chose the former. I chose quitting my addictions. I chose taking the path that has led me to this page, this story and a new understanding.

I have some other stories to share on my journey and I hope you will stick around to hear them. I have been fortunate to get this far in the dream called life. I have seen what is ahead and am very thankful for the awakening. I don't think you will want to miss the ending, I know I don't.

INTRODUCTION

Calm down Chicken Little, the sky is not falling and the world is not coming to an end.

Apocalypse

Just what does Apocalypse mean anyway? Where did the term come from? Does the concept apply to the end of time; end of the world; end of humanity; the end of me? Or, does it mean something entirely different?

Most word usage in Western Civilization comes from the Greek and/or Latin languages. If you are ever curious about what something means use the dictionary and/or a good online encyclopedia like Wikipedia. Much of the factual information in this book comes from Wikipedia and the dictionary.

The earliest use and meaning of the word apocalypse, comes from the Greek (*apokalypsis*), meaning to "lift the veil" or "revelation." The term implies that something important is hidden and/or sacred and is revealed only to a privileged or special group when a task is accomplished and the "time" is appropriate. In other words, a revelation comes to the individual when the "time" or "age" of the individual is over, because the individual has matured to a new understanding and therefore begins a new age. A revelation brings on "a new age" and new responsibility for the individual. Simply stated, the formerly uninformed (ignorant) person passes through a "rite of passage" and now being enlightened dies (metaphorically) to his former self and enters his new age. I know this only too well.

The elders in most cultures hold that knowledge is sacred and is not to be shared with the masses or the "vulgar". Sacred knowledge can only be given to an "initiate" who makes a commitment, goes through a ritual and passes some test. The English term "initiate" comes from the Latin word "*initium*" meaning "an entrance" or "a beginning". The term originally developed out of ancient tribal (shaman) initiations or "rites of passage" rituals. Subsequently, all sacred knowledge was held in mystery schools throughout the world and much of it in "secret societies." Once initiated the formerly ignorant person now possesses inner knowledge, which ends his uninformed "age" or "time" and he now becomes filled with the light of truth and is called "enlightened." The term "initiate" literally means, "to go within." This is what is meant by the Biblical parable, "When I was a child, I spoke as a child and acted as a child, but when I became a man (matured) I put away childish things." Revelation is ultimately "going within." It is very personal. It is an apocalypse.

While most of us have never gone through a formal rite of passage or have never enrolled in a mystery school, most all of us have had an "ah-ha" experience at least once in their lives. Out of the blue you just "get it." Get what you ask? "It". When asked to define "it" you can't, but you know without question that what you got was totally right if not profoundly right. Often when one "gets it" his life is never the same again. It has happened to me on more than one occasion.

In the movie The Matrix, Neo was presented with the choice of taking the blue or red pill? As Morpheus cautioned, "Once you take the red pill you can't go back." Once you "get it" you can't go back. Go back to what? To the world as it was. Everything changes. When one becomes aware or understands something on an intuitive level it is often non-verbal and not reversible. It's the "Oh My God" experience. That my friend is an apocalypse and just a little taste of what December 21, 2012 is all about.

Revelation has to do with the mind, not the body.

Nowhere in ancient literature, up and until the establishment of the Catholic Church, do we get that revelation is about physical world changes. The Church gave us this misinformation. Not until the

"Christians" began writing about the "end of days" around 300 AD do we get mention of catastrophic changes to the Earth in prophecy. The early apocalyptic writings were more of a hope for liberation from the evils of Roman oppression than "God's Will" for the planet and men in the future.

As ancient philosophy gradually gave way to Church dogma and creed (rules), we begin to see the "mystery" turning into a fundamental literalism. From the "Dark Ages" (500CE to 1500CE) the church decided what was true and false and truth became literal. As truth becomes literal, so do traditions until the mystery is lost altogether. Debating the Church in the middle ages would likely have gotten you killed. Not a very good idea today. Most of humanity did what they were told. Very few could read or write and Church services were in Latin. Speculation regarding the age to come and the hope for the "chosen people" more than anything else caused the rise and influenced the development of apocalyptic literature.

Our sense of the apocalyptic today comes from the Church's misinterpretation of the Greek phrase *"apolalupsic eschaton"* which originally meant revelation coming at the "beginning" of a new age, not at the end. The Church's literal version was "judgment" coming at the "end of the age", which was John's message in the Book of Revelations. Instead of revelation being a personal thing, the writers of the New Testament began to refer to revelation as coming only from God and apocalypse meaning the "end of time" for all but a special few. One thousand years of dogma became hard to refute especially at the risk of one's life.

So, what does all this have to do with December 21, 2012?

Everything!

The book you are reading is divided into three parts: Part I – The Undoing, Part II – The Preparation and Part III – The Transformation. It will become clear as you read that this format is as much an initiation as information.

As sure as you are reading this page a Winter Solstice will come on December 21, 2012. Much has been written and much will be written as that date approaches. Most of what you will hear and read will be doomsday stuff.

Is that date peculiar only to the Mayan Calendar? No. Are the Mayans saying the world ends in cataclysm? No. Are there any other issues, historical or otherwise influencing this date? Yes. Since it is an astrological event, what do astrologers say? Rather than Doomsday, could there be some other revelation intended? Absolutely!

There is much to be learned and many changes are about to take place. Many will seize the opportunity and many will go on with not as much as a hick-up on December 22, 2012. Will the world end? No. Will it be different? Yes. How different? That is up to you. You control the outcome. The outcome doesn't control you.

By the way, this is not about the outer world. It never was. It's about you.

It's a revelation, an apocalyptic revelation.

CONTENTS

Acknowledgment iii
Biographical Sketch v
Introduction xiii

PART ONE   **THE UNDOING** 1

Chapter One   The Gordian Knot 3
Chapter Two   In The Beginning 21
Chapter Three   Where God Comes From 35
Chapter Four   The Gnostics 59
Chapter Five   Deceptions and Myths of the Bible 79

PART TWO   **THE PREPARATION** 85

Chapter Six   Consciousness 87
Chapter Seven   Awareness 105
Chapter Eight   Love Is All There Is 123
Chapter Nine   Meditation 133

PART THREE   **TRANSFORMATION** 141

Chapter Ten   Resurrection is of the Mind 143
Chapter Eleven   Awaken 151
Chapter Twelve   Nonduality 159
Chapter Thirteen   East and West 167
Chapter Fourteen   Transformation 175

Final Thoughts   A New World 187
Bibliography   191

PART ONE

THE UNDOING

Chapter One

THE GORDIAN KNOT

Wake up!

The world stands on the threshold of a consciousness revolution. Make no mistake; pressure is building everywhere on planet Earth. Greed and avarice have nearly bankrupted the world's financial institutions. The eco-system is crippled and depression is building in the hearts and minds of the people. While it is dark, it is likely to get much darker before the dawn.

Is December 21, 2012 an ending, or a beginning? It has to be one or the other. Will it be catastrophic?

I believe it will be positive regardless of the physical changes that are predicted. One way or another a worldwide change in consciousness has to happen. The planet and the population are suffering. If the world does not change the way it treats its neighbors and its eco-system the outcome will be more perilous than imagined. It will require a worldwide crisis to get the world's attention. What that crisis will look like is anyone's guess. Would you agree that one way or the other something has to give?

Before we can move on we need to take a long look at where we have been and get very clear as to where we want to go. The world stands at the brink of moving into a golden age of love, compassion and humility or destroy itself through fear. What are your priorities as a person, a nation and a planet? All civilizations fail from within, not from without. What once was true for nation states is now true for the entire planet. Today we are a global society. We all have a lot in common. No one is special. Power and disregard for human life has brought empires down before and will again. There is a line in Pete Seeger's song "Where have all the Flowers Gone?" that simply says, "When will we ever learn"? Indeed, when?

In 1956 MGM released a classic science fiction movie entitled "The Forbidden Planet." In that movie a civilization on Planet Altair IV, called the Krell, had disappeared and a team of scientists was sent to determine why? It seems that the entire race had disappeared some 200,000 years ago but the physical communities were still functioning. As it turned out the race had advanced to such a degree that they had overcome all resistance to matter and had created an automated infrastructure. Everything was running on an energy source that could not be determined. So, where did all the people go?

It was determined that the race had advanced to the point that they eliminated all obstacles to survival except for one. Fear. They had not overcome the fear that their creation could fail. As they fed into that fear they created an invisible force, which did in fact turn on them and destroyed their society. Their collective conscious was so strong that while the cities remained the people were eliminated. Does that sound similar to what we have created today with our worldwide banking crisis and global warming?

The current global crisis is a product of greed and outright denial of the consequences. The question today is will collective world consciousness create a collective world catharsis or a collective world solution. Carl Jung said there is a collective consciousness throughout humanity. That is why the same invention can occur in different parts of the world at the same time and psychics predict similar events in different parts of the World at the same time.

Could collective conscious bring down a country or a planet? Could this be what the Maya and a number of worldwide Oracles have been saying for centuries? Are we looking at a tipping point toward catastrophe or a golden age? Isn't it clear that we can never return to business as usual? It should be obvious that more of the same is not a solution but a crisis waiting to happen on a planetary scale.

Progress is initially measured by how much an individual or nation accumulates and then how they treat their neighbors. But accumulation never seems to be enough. What's enough? All empires fail because their answer to this question is: everything! Consciousness expansion is the key to progress and at the base of all great societies. But consciousness without compassion is a formula for disaster. Most empires get lost along the way. They fall asleep to what was originally intended. Societies give too much energy to the objective at the expense of the subjective. All failures are based on an obsession with materialism.

Taking a look at the lives of people around the industrialized world there seems to be a lot of unhappiness. Why? As a country the United States has the highest standard of living in the world. Its citizens are among the best educated, fed and housed in the world. Yet greed and disregard for the environment has brought about a depression in the economy and a tragedy in the ecology, not only in the US but also around the globe. What is going to make it any different?

Some say it will take a worldwide catastrophe to get the world's attention; that we must work together or suffer the consequences. Some say that this time is fast approaching in the form of a "new age." There is no doubt that a dilemma has been placed on the doorstep of humanity. What do you think will happen? What is your role in this? Your opinion is very important. Your world depends on it.

The Gordian knot

The Gordian knot is a legend associated with Alexander the Great. It is a metaphor for solving a seemingly unsolvable problem through using a "bold stroke". In this metaphor we see a certain complicated knot tying an ox-cart to its yoke (most likely a metaphor for tying the ruling priestly class to control) in the town square of Gordium in Western Turkey.

The legend stated that whoever untied the knot would become king of Gordium. As the legend goes, in 333 BCE, while wintering at Gordium, Alexander attempted to untie the knot. He could not find the ends of the knot to unravel it. Therefore with a stroke of his sword (to be subsequently known as the "*Alexandrian Solution*") the ends of the knot were revealed, the puzzle solved and Alexander was crowned king. Subsequently, an oracle from Greece prophesied that whoever untied the knot would become king of Asia. Alexander went on to conquer the known world from the Mediterranean to the Indian Ocean thus fulfilling the prophecy. Whether the knot was cut or manipulated is unimportant. The mystery was solved, the aristocracy broken and the hero rewarded.

This is a tale known by both the literate and the illiterate as it was written down and passed along for hundreds of years. So, it is both a fact and a metaphor. Did an actual knot exist or was it a story invented to justify the ends? Maybe the knot was a total invention?

We all have a Gordian knot

First comes the recognition that there is something tying you down with no perceivable way of getting free. Upon recognition (by the very few) comes the effort to free oneself. This is the hero's journey. Alexander could not move on until the puzzle was solved. Have you recognized your personal problem let alone the world's problem? It took me many years to admit there was a problem in my life and another 30 years of whacking away at it. I think it's called denial! From my personal experience I can tell you that it will take a bold stroke to find the ends of the knot and unravel the mystery of who you are. It is the hero's journey. It is the greatest journey ever undertaken. The stakes are high. The reward is peace of mind.

The good news is, it can be done! The hero's journey, as Joseph Campbell calls it, is the surrendering of one's "self" to something bigger than oneself. At first you will not know what that is but it eventually dawns. The hero's journey leads to the revelation that unveils the meaning of life. It is the greatest journey of them all. It is the only reason you are in your body. It is a cycle of going out and going in.

By the way, answers to your problem are never found "out there". They are only found in you, on the way home. It has taken me a lifetime to get this but it was worth the trip. I now have a grasp on the mystery and my role in it is to help others find their way home if they want it bad enough. I cannot simply give you the answer; it is up to you to find it for yourself. First you must recognize there is a knot in your life that needs undoing. Is it alcohol, drugs, relationships, money, security, fear, family, the church etc.

We are on the threshold of a new age. We have a great opportunity to cut the knot that binds us to lifetimes of ignorance. Have you had it with your circumstances yet? I can show you the path and I can hand you the sword but I cannot decide for you. You must make that choice on your own. To me it's simple: nothing changes if nothing changes! For me I choose freedom. It wasn't always so. I had clearly chosen slavery all my life but called it being successful.

If you are truly happy with what you have created then you have nothing to learn. For those of you who decide to take the bold stroke toward enlightenment, I guarantee you will be rewarded. You will be on freedom's train and out of slavery. For those of you who do not take advantage of this time and the ending of the current age, be at peace in your sleep. You can either awaken from the dream of separation (which is your biggest problem) or continue to sleep in the illusion of time and space. This is what December 21, 2012 is all about. It's a wake up call!

First we must undo what we have done before we can prepare for the transition into the reality of who we really are. You may "get it" right away or it may take some time. Whatever it takes, it's worth it! The important thing for now is to get real about what you want. Do you want to wake up from a dream of unreality and enter the new age of enlightenment or continue to be challenged in the illusion of your own making? The choice is yours and it is only yours. No one can choose for you and there is no one out there to save you.

Remember what Morpheus said to Neo in the Matrix movie? "Taking the red pill exposes this apparent reality as false (as the matrix) but also remember that in taking the red pill there is no turning back. The blue pill is a sleeping pill. So, which is it, red or blue?"

It has taken me half a lifetime just to become aware that "apparent reality" is the matrix, but there is a way out. Commitment is the red pill and there is no turning back. There is no one out there who can do it for you. That is part of the mystery you will learn later on but you have help. Every recovering alcoholic knows this to be an absolute fact. Right? I've tried God, booze, drugs, sex, psychedelics, books and gurus. Guess what, the answers were not out there. I found my answers on the way home. I found them in the undoing not the doing. That is the hero's journey. Guess what? You are the hero of your play.

The Power of Myth

All the world's myths point to the transformation of consciousness. Consciousness, your "perception about yourself" and the world around you, is created and changed either by trials or by illuminating revelations or both. The purpose of life is trials and revelations. The hero, you, launches himself/herself into the journey of life in an attempt to find his/her real self. The problem is the illusion seems so real that we get sidetracked along the way. Then some revelation occurs to us and we move on or we are too asleep to see it.

"Revelation" is the key. We can only move forward through revelation. Look at your life, I'll bet you have had several revelations. Did you move on, or fall deeper into sleep? Those who get stuck and can't move on become life's casualties. You know them. You may be one. The problem with revelation is once you have one, and recognize it, can you stay with it long enough before you fall asleep again?

It all has to do with clarity. How clear were you when you got the revelation. It may take several attempts to wake you up but one thing's for sure; you will keep trying to wake up until you do. You can't help it;

it's why you're here. How many lifetimes do you want to invest in this process is the question? Somewhere inside you, you know this is true.

The opportunity in the next few years is phenomenal because of accelerated energy. Now more than ever you must be careful whom you hang with. Put yourself in situations that will evoke your higher nature. Don't put yourself into temptation but deliver yourself from evil. Look for the light and the light will respond. The dawning of the new age is an opportunity unlike any you have ever had to move out of the darkness forever. Untie the knot and become king of your universe. You can break the chain of birth to death to birth again.

The Age of Aquarius

December 21, is the winter solstice for 2009. Does it, in any way, tie to the Age of Aquarius, the Mayan Calendar or prophecy?

The Age of Aquarius is the upcoming new astrological age of the zodiac. We are currently in the twilight of Pisces. Each astrological age is approximately 2,000 years long but there are various methods of calculating this length that may yield longer or shorter time spans. In sun-sign astrology the first sign in the entire zodiac is Aquarius followed by Capricorn, Gemini, Cancer, Leo, Virgo, Libra, Scorpio, Sagittarius and ending the cycle with Pisces. Once Pisces passes, the Age of Aquarius begins the precession all over again. The entire cycle takes some 26,000 years to complete. No one knows for certain when an age begins or ends. We do know that this is a new age and a new cycle. It won't happen again for 26,000 years!

Astrological ages exist as a result of the precession of the equinoxes (see Wikipedia for explanation). The stars and constellations appear to slowly rotate around the Earth independent of the daily and annual movements of the Earth on its axis and around the Sun. This slow movement takes slightly less than 26,000 years to complete one cycle. Approximately every 2,160 years the sun's position at the time of the Vernal Equinox (usually March 21st) will have moved into a new zodiacal constellation. According to astrological calculations the Age of Aquarius should arrive full force in the year 2,600CE. The "dawning" of the Age of Aquarius could be as much as 700 years sooner. We are in the dawning now.

Some astrologers believe that Ages affect individual human beings based on their birth dates. Others believe that Ages correlate to the rise and fall of mighty civilizations and cultural tendencies. Aquarius traditionally "rules" electricity, computers, flight, democracy, freedom, humanitarianism, idealists, modernization, rebels and rebellion, mental disease, nervous disorders and astrology. These factors give rise to the belief among many astrologers that we have been in the Aquarian Age for several hundred years considering our planetary history (the American Revolution, the Industrial Revolution, discovery of electricity, the Internet, great material advancement and the psychological issues connected with materialism).

Projections are for the humanizing of mankind and a future peaceful contact with extraterrestrials. The words enlightenment and the expansion of consciousness appear in most of these astrological predictions. World turmoil is always the situation when two Ages collide. Rome was at the height of power at the dawning of Pisces and fell. What the world is experiencing now would be in concert with the ending of Pisces and the beginning of Aquarius. Many will be called to wake up in advance of others and be recognized as leaders in the new age. It happens in every age. Buddha was a great teacher at the dawning of the age of Pisces. Jesus or the Jesus story at the peak.

On the other hand some astrologers see the planet entering into a dark time where secretive power-hungry elites will seek absolute power over others. Families will dissolve completely. Other negative influences of Aquarius are the dumbing down of humanity through the media and the Internet. It may be a time when Corporations take control of economies, governments and religions.

Ray Grasse provides a guide for the Aquarian Age analogous to a travel guide for someone entering a foreign land. He suggests leaving room for silence in your life. Create a center in your life be it in your home or with a group. The objective of the silence is to connect with the absolute. Give up attachment to the material and focus on the living, organic substance of the planet. Maintain a compassionate heart and take control of your everyday attitudes. Grasse cautions, "How do we know the Age of Aquarius will be a utopia or an Orwellian nightmare?" It will be one or the other. No more status quo.

Perhaps the poet who wrote the opening lines to the song, The Age of Aquarius for the 1967 musical Hair, had it right when he wrote, "This is the dawning of the Age of Aquarius." He also announced the start date of the new Age when he wrote: "When the moon is in the seventh house and Jupiter aligns with Mars. Then peace will guide the planets, and love will steer the stars." Actually this did happen on February 14, 2009 – Valentine's Day!

The Mayan (a Mesoamerican, Pre Columbian, Central American Culture) like many other primitive cultures governed their reality on the alignment of the stars. They were obsessed with time. They wrote about events preceding their time, with stunning accuracy, and prophesized many other events during their lifetime and the future which have come true. The Mayan had three calendars more accurate than those in use today.

Some believe the Maya called for the end of time with their long calendar ending on December 21, 2012. The Maya were not saying the world would end in some cataclysm. That is a misinterpretation. The date is simply the beginning of a new long count calendar (26,000 years) but there are serious issues to be considered; very serious issues for all of mankind. Solar Flares will be at their peak in late 2012.

So, what needs undoing?

Symbols, Words, and Concepts:

Because we use symbols, words and concepts to establish beliefs, let's take a look at the major concepts that feed into belief. You will need to refer to these from time to time.

Cosmology – The study of the Universe in its totality and by extension, humanities place in it. The Universe comprises everything that physically exists: space, time, matter and energy as well as the issues of momentum, physical laws and constants that govern these issues. Cosmology is a relatively new term but the study of the Universe has a long history involving philosophy, esotericism, mythology and religion. Cosmology is both objective and subjective at the same time.

Philosophy – The study of general and fundamental subjective problems concerning matters such as existence, knowledge, values, reason, mind and language. Philosophy is distinguished from other ways of addressing these questions by its critical, generally systematic approach and its reliance on reasoned argument. Philosophy comes from the Greek (*philosophia*), which literally translates, to "the love of wisdom".

Esotericism- The word derives from the Greek (*esoterikos*) meaning "within" thus pertaining to the inward or mystical. In scholarly literature the term designates a series of historically related subjects including Gnosticism, magic, astrology, alchemy, Rosicrucianism, Christian Theosophy, Mesmerism, and Spiritualism. Esoteric knowledge is available to a narrow circle of "enlightened", "initiated" or specially educated people. The antonym of esoteric is exoteric which is knowledge well known to the public at large (outer temple teachings).

Mysticism - The pursuit or communion with, identity with, or conscious awareness of an ultimate reality (absolute reality), divinity, spiritual truth or God through direct experience or awareness. Mysticism may be dualistic (from the Latin duo meaning two) maintaining a distinction between the self and the divine, or may be non-dualistic implying that things may be distinct even if not being separate.

Mythology – Refers to the study of myths or a body of myths. The academic use of the term does not presuppose truth or falsity. A myth is conventionally defined as a sacred narrative explaining how the world and mankind came to be in their present form.

Religion – A system of human thought which usually includes a set of narratives, symbols, beliefs and practices that give meaning to the individual's experiences of life through reference to a higher power, deity or ultimate truth. Religion is commonly identified by prayer, ritual, meditation, music and art and generally reflects society and political views.

It may focus on specific supernatural, metaphysical, and moral claims about reality, which usually yields a set of laws, ethics and a particular lifestyle. Religion also encompasses ancestral or cultural traditions, writings, history, and mythology as well as personal faith and religious experience.

Belief – A psychological, cultural state in which an individual holds a proposition or premise to be true or false. The term belief is used differently in philosophy.

Epistemology - The philosophical study of belief and knowledge. What is needed in order for us to have a belief or knowledge? In a word – Justification.

Knowledge – A concept held through experience. **Belief** is an abstraction about that knowledge. Belief has no usefulness without knowledge. Belief assumes a subject (the believer) and an object of the belief (the proposition). Knowledge is mostly based on dualistic perception.

Science surfaces to prove that which is perceived and real must be measurable. If the proposition is flawed to begin with then no proof is possible or required and all beliefs are labeled nebulous. This is called the quantum argument, or people believe what they have been told because there is no quantifiable evidence to propose otherwise.

Ask yourself two questions: "If there were no language, could there be any belief"? If there could be no observation, could there be any proof? How would you know? Language and observation are inventions of the mind to validate the status quo. How reliable is the mind?

Truth – The term truth has no single definition about which a majority of professional philosophers and scholars agree. Truths are independent of our beliefs. Thinking doesn't make a proposition true or false. Truth is subjective and relative.

Persuasion to a majority "opinion" creates a truth. It is a rhetorical or consensual truth. Religions are great examples of socially constructed truth therefore giving rise to a socially constructed reality. The reality is neither true nor false but what the group has agreed upon.

Fact – Derives from the Latin (*factum*) meaning a pragmatic truth, which is a statement that can be observed, checked, confirmed and proven. Opinions on the other hand cannot be observed, checked, confirmed or proved by an acceptable and established method. Using the term "fact" often bring with it the term "truth". It was once held that the Earth was flat or the Earth was the center of the solar system. These were facts and truths for that time but proven incorrect with time. In fact these propositions were not factual but dogmatic.

How can anything that is subject to "change" be true? It cannot! Ultimately nothing is true or false (objectively), only perceived and agreed upon to be either.

Facts are proven wrong every day. The only truth or fact would be absolute and unchanging. That is not possible in a world constructed from the five senses. All facts in the objective world are postulates from theories. There is nothing absolute in physics or metaphysics. Quantum physics suggests that the mere act of observation can change a fact! Nothing is factual only contrived.

Reality – the state of things as they actually exist which takes in both being and not being. Both propositions support a reality. In physical science, existence is often restricted to being only which quantum physics suggests is false. What about dark matter? It holds all perceived reality together yet has no reality of its own! Which is true, that which allows or that which is perceived?

The term "reality" first appeared in the English language from the Latin (*realitatem*) language in 1550 CE. It was originally a legal term applied to fixed property e.g. "real" estate.

On a much broader and more subjective level, private experiences, curiosity, inquiry and selectivity involved in personal interpretation of events shapes reality as seen by one and only one individual and is hence called phenomenological from the German (*phainomenon*) meaning "that which appears". While this form of reality might be common to others as well, it could at times also be unique to oneself as to never be experienced or agreed upon by anyone else. Much of the kind of experience deemed spiritual occurs on this level of reality.

Some schools of Buddhism hold that reality is something void of description, the formless which forms all illusions is *maya*. Buddhists hold that we can only discuss objects, which are not reality itself, and that nothing can be said of reality, which is true in any absolute sense. Everything is maya or illusion. Any discussion about reality would be an illusion. Anything that can be named is not real.

The Buddha...

Believe not because some old manuscripts are produced.

Believe not because it is your national belief.

Believe not because you have been made to believe from childhood.

Rather, reason truth out and after you have analyzed it, then if you find it will do good to one and all, believe it, live up to it and help others live up to it.

At large both science and philosophy spend most of their time discussing reality by saying what it is NOT rather than what it is. Again, it is all theory. At the end of the day most quantum scientists and philosophers agree that perception is the only reality.

Other knots

It has been my experience that cultural "belief" comes down to an acceptable definition of certain words and concepts. Belief seems to be a comfort zone of concepts dictated by one's environment. Words and concepts can only point the way but cannot resolve anything. When a word or concept is mentioned what is your comfort zone about the word? Do you have a definition that you feel comfortable with? What does your gut tell you? What is your belief? Where did that belief or comfort zone come from? Belief is very personal.

I have prepared a list of words that have given me the most difficulty in my life. As I have read, researched and talked to others I find these words seem to be common problems for most people. There isn't a single subject under the sun that two people would agree on completely because of perception. That is as it should be because there is no one truth in "relativity." Perceived reality is relative and therefore subject to argument. When it comes to developing a new cosmology or changing the status quo, the following will need to be considered as it binds you to your current belief and self-concept.

Your definitions create your world.

Take a piece of paper and write down your perception (belief) about these words. After you read this book, come back and see if you have changed your perception. You may want to add some other words to the list as you read. This will become a mind-altering experience as you first see where you are today, then after reading this book see where you are in the "future."

- God
- Christ
- Anti-Christ
- Spirit
- Holy Spirit

- Presence
- Son of God
- Consciousness
- Understanding
- Knowing
- Awareness
- Enlightenment
- Dreaming
- Waking Up
- Projection
- Perception
- Reality
- Illusion
- Good
- Evil
- Idol
- Free Will
- Belief
- Faith
- Denial
- Love
- Fear
- Pain

PART ONE - THE UNDOING

- Suffering
- Special
- Thought
- Sin
- Guilt
- Shame
- Resistance
- Joy
- Peace
- Happiness
- Acceptance
- Pleasure
- Desire
- Trust
- Mind
- Body
- Ego
- Attack
- Defense
- Victim
- Judgment
- Grievance
- Anger

- Competition
- Sacrifice
- Forgiveness
- Salvation
- Miracle
- Subjective
- Objective
- Content
- Context
- Reality
- Form
- Linear
- Non-Linear
- Quantum
- Boundary
- Seeing
- Vision
- Light
- Darkness
- Time
- Now
- Eternity
- Doing

PART ONE - THE UNDOING

- Being
- Death
- Birth
- Resurrection
- Ascension
- Reincarnation
- Prayer
- Meditation
- Revelation
- Witnessing
- Heaven
- Hell
- Sickness
- Healing
- Insight
- Intuition
- Freedom
- Dualism

CHAPTER TWO

IN THE BEGINNING

In the "BEGINNING" there was a "BIG VOID" called "THE BIG NOTHING".

Suddenly, there was a "BIG EXPLOSION", called the "BIG BANG."

In about "six days" you wouldn't believe all the stuff that happened: water, land, sky, stars, a bunch of laid back animals, a really great "GARDEN" and "THE FIRST GUY". Man, what a week!

In the GARDEN the FIRST GUY was "put to work" naming thing. Not an easy job without a vocabulary. You try coming up with all those names. After naming most everything in sight the FIRST GUY felt a little tired and fell asleep. When he woke up he expressed a sense of loneliness to THE BIG GUY. That very evening THE BIG GUY breaks the FIRST GUY'S ribs! (Probably for complaining about his job) and by morning there's A SECOND GUY hanging around looking much like the THE FIRST GUY with some added and missing parts.

After a few days...

FIRST GUY: "So, what should we call each other?" (Assume the vocabulary).

SECOND GUY: "You are the first guy, right, and I am the SECOND GUY, right?

FIRST GUY: "I suppose so. So, what's your name?"

SECOND GUY: "Well, since I am the SECOND GUY, why not call me Adamam." Get it?" Add-a-mam!

They both start to chuckle. (The first humor)

All of a sudden THE BIG GUY, seeing no humor in any of this, interrupts: "Wait a minute, just wait a minute, there is something you both need to know and quick. One of you is a "man" the other is a "wo-man". While I like the Adamam idea, it's just not going to work in the "future". But I like the Ad-a-man idea. "So, FIRST GUY, your name is Adam." SECOND GUY, your name is Eve, which is short for lady from the evening.

Everyone was happy and life was good. However, Eve began questioning Adam about his job.

EVE: "All you do is "name things", is that right? You mean, like all day long just naming things? What happens when you run out of things to name? Might think about getting a real job."

ADAM: "I'm sure glad I have someone to think for me. That must be what a wo-man is for?"

Meanwhile, back in THE GARDEN Adam is busy naming stuff when he bumps into a "TALKING SNAKE".

SNAKE: "Say, Adam, I hear you might be looking for a good job"?

ADAM: "What's a good job? You've been talking to Eve, right"?

SNAKE: "How about a one-of-a-kind talking snake act? Believe me, there isn't another one on Earth. We could take it on the road, probably make millions. We could...uh...could...uh...we could... sell... snake oil!"

ADAM: "Well, why not. Eve's been on me about getting a real job. By the way, what's a million?"

SNAKE: "Don't concern yourself Adam, you'll get it soon enough. Before we get started, what say we do lunch? I just happen to know this groovy place over by the "tree of knowledge, and...."

ADAM: Interrupting Snake, "You're not suggesting the BIG GUY'S apples are you?"

SNAKE: Ignoring the question, "Maybe we better see if Eve has had lunch yet?"

Both Adam and Snake move along the path toward the "Tree" when Eve appears and asks where they are going.

ADAM: "Eve, I was just thinking about what you said, you know, the job thing? And up pops this talking snake. This snake has this great idea and a job offer that could last us forever."

EVE: " So, what's in it for the snake?"

ADAM: "Oh, he's just wanting to help us "out."

EVE: "Out of what, Adam?"

ADAM: "Something about being on our own. Having our own business. Making our own decisions. Stuff like that."

EVE: Gazing at the snake and in a somewhat seductive voice says, "So, tell me more Big Boy."

SNAKE: "Eve, I can see you have a head for business. Adam and I were about to have lunch. Would you like to join us?"

EVE: "Sure, what's for lunch?"

SNAKE: "Apples! Not just any apples mind you. These are very special apples from The Tree of Knowledge of Good and Evil. You'll need knowledge in the business world."

ADAM: "Not the BIG GUY'S apples. He told us they were off limits."

SNAKE: "Look Adam, there's always risk going into business for yourself. You know what they say, No risk, no gain? Besides, the BIG GUY only walks here in the cool of the evening and it's the middle of the day. We're only talking one apple. Hell man, the way things grow around here the damned apple will probably grow back by evening!"

ADAM: "OK, OK, I get it, I get it. Let's eat!"

As Adam reaches for the apple, snake looks at Adam, winks and nods towards Eve.

SNAKE: "Ever hear of ladies first, Adam?"

ADAM: "Not really, but why not?"

SNAKE: "Just think, one bite and you'll both know everything the BIG GUY knows. That's why He doesn't want you to eat the apple. He's afraid you will go into competition with him."

With that final bit of encouragement, Eve takes a bite and hands the apple to Adam.

Almost immediately the clouds roll in complete with thunder, lightening, rain and hail. Never a good sign in any GARDEN.

Snake disappears under a rock. Adam and Eve grab some fig leaves to keep the hail off and a rumbling voice begins to speak:

BIG GUY: "Adam, have you been eating my apples?"

SNAKE: In a whispering voice, "I thought He knew everything, why is he asking questions?"

Another bolt of lightning and the snake slithers deeper into the darkness.

ADAM: "Look, it's just one apple and besides Eve did it first."

BIG GUY: "I see, you've already learned passing the buck. What else have you learned?"

ADAM: "Eve and I have decided to make a go of it in the world. We're going into business with snake. Sometimes you have to do what you have to do. You of …uh…all persons…uh…all things…uh…well, you can surely understand that?"

BIG GUY: "I'm not very happy with you guys right now, but yes you can come back when you get sick and tired or the world. All that's required is that you give up your snake friend, get past the two guards at the GARDEN gate and eat from the "Tree of Life".

ADAM: "Really?"

BIG GUY: "Hey, it's your choice. It's called FREE WILL."

So, off they went. Adam, Eve and the Snake.

A short way out of the GARDEN they hear what sounds like music and laughter coming over the dimly lit horizon to the East. About an hour into their journey they see a sign, which says, "Land of Nod- This Way".

Soon they arrive in Nod and in short order the memory of the garden, the big guy, magical trees bearing magical fruit and the easy life fades.

EVE: "Adam, did you ever see so much snake oil in your life?"

ADAM: "You know Eve, I was just thinking the same thing. We need a new gimmick, maybe adding a little food coloring to the snake oil?

Don't worry, I'm working on an idea for a book about an garden, a snake and………."

And they all fell happily asleep forever.

MEDIEVAL TO MODERN WORLDVIEWS

Our Modern worldview began with the collapse of the medieval worldview (approximately 1600 C.E.)

The Church's influence on the worldview began with the collapse of the Roman Empire in the 4th Century. The Church's domination of the worldview began in the 5th Century and lasted until the collapse of the medieval period during the 16th Century. That's 1,000 years of church dominated worldview! It is an age of superstition, legends folklore and ignorance.

TheDarkAges–500 to 1600CE. (The Period of Unenlightenment.) The church told the world what to think, and the people accepted this view without question. Death or torture was the penalty for not going along with the official doctrine.

Before 1500 C.E. the dominant world-view in Europe, as well as other civilizations, was organic. People lived in small, cohesive communities and experienced nature in terms of organic relationships. Spiritual and material phenomenon were inter related. The needs of the individual were subordinate to the community. The framework for this organic, Western world-view rested on two authorities – Aristotle and the Church.

Thomas Aquinas combined Aristotle's comprehensive system of nature with Christian theology and ethics, which established the conceptual framework that remained unquestioned throughout the Middle Ages.

The Italian Renaissance began in the 14th Century with the revival of literature and art. The previous worldview begins to be questioned, but not seriously altered until the 17th Century.

Up to the 16th Century

1. We did not know a single human organ or its function.

2. Had no idea of the biology of plant life.

3. Thunderstorms were the result of an angry God.

4. Nature and human life were defined in strictly religious terms.

5. The Earth was the center of the universe. (A stage upon which man either won or lost Salvation.) Everything – famine, disease, floods, wars were a test of faith. Satan, an invention of the Church, orchestrated all of it in an attempt to spoil our bid for eternal happiness.

6. The Church was the sole Gatekeeper. It controlled all written materials and records. Man had to rely on the Church for defining everything. The populace of the Christian world was kept ignorant on purpose. No one could read or write except the priesthood. The individual of the day, having "sinned," could not go directly to God for forgiveness, but only to the Church.

Causes for the collapse of the worldview in the 16th Century are numerous. Among others, the following are significant

1. Expanding trade brought word of new cultures and outlooks that challenged the medieval cosmology.

2. Excesses and extremes of the churchmen eventually undermined the church's credibility.

3. The invention of the printing press, which put the Bible and Books of Antiquity into the population, which led to the Protestant Reformation.

4. A new kind of thinker – Copernicus, Galileo, and Kepler – directly challenged the church's dogma on the structure of the solar system, and even mankind's place in the universe.

5. As the Renaissance and the Enlightenment emerged, God was pushed further and further from everyday consciousness.

So, with the collapse of the 1,000-year-old paradigm, what could man believe in? If the church was wrong, who could be trusted and by what authority? By the 16th Century Western Civilization was stuck in a no-man's-land between worldviews.

By the end of the 17th Century, the West (west of Suez) was proceeding toward science and technology, which would revolutionize civilization. The Western perception of God was about to dramatically change. Up to this time the world was primarily a civilization dependent on agriculture. We now begin to see the development of cities, societies and commerce connected with the production of goods and services.

The Enlightenment or "Age of Reason" introduced ideas that would forever change the way we look at God and ourselves. The scientific revolution began with Nicolas Copernicus who overthrew the age-old Biblical view that the earth was the center of the universe. He knew his studies would not be accepted by the church and were not released until his death in 1543 C.E., and only then as theory. Copernicus was followed by Kepler and then by Galileo who validated Copernicus work as placing the sun at the center of the solar system and the earth as one of many planets in orbit around the sun. This broke the back of church authority and ushered in the Age of Reason. (Galileo was the first to combine scientific experiment with mathematics and is considered the father of modern science).

The following are a few of the many philosopher/scientists creating the paradigm shift we experience today:

Rene Descartes – A mathematician and founder of "Cartesian" philosophy (cause and effect), which is still the basis of modern science today. He was the first to apply numbers to geometrical figures thus founding analytic geometry. The belief in the certainty of scientific knowledge lies at the basis of Cartesian philosophy. All things can be proven using mathematical analysis. (20th Century physics would disprove this assumption).

He believed the material universe was a machine and nothing else. There was no purpose, life or spirituality in matter. Nature worked according to mechanical laws. This drastic change in the image of nature from organism to machine began the idea of manifest destiny (masculine) to dominate nature (feminine) and began the male exploitation of the planet.

He believed that by "conceiving" of God, God exists. However, God is primarily an intellectual state. God has nothing to do with mystery or faith, which were primitive states of perception. Civilized man had outgrown these elementary ideas. Descartes represents the birth of rationalism where the mind can find an answer to anything. Cerebral activity is the source of all ideas. (*Cogito ergo sum*). I think therefore I am was ultimately the only reality he could establish as ultimate.

While Descartes created the conceptual framework for 17th Century science, it was Isaac Newton, born in England in 1642 CE (the same year that Galileo died) who developed the complete mathematical formulation of the mechanistic view of nature thus accomplishing a grand synthesis of the works of Copernicus, Kepler, Bacon, Galileo, and Descartes.

Isaac Newton – Newton had a grasp of mathematic far beyond his predecessors. He invented calculus, which Einstein said was "perhaps the greatest advance in thought that a single individual was ever privileged to make". Newton's starting point was mechanics not mathematics. Newton was interested in explaining the physical universe with God as an essential part of it. God is a continuation of the natural, physical order. Not above or below but a part of.

Newton introduced the proposition that a gravitational force governed the world and the universe. Gravity was the force that governs all moving particles not God. This seriously compromised the absolute sovereignty of God and the Church.

It was gravity that kept things in their proper place, thus preventing chaos. It took an intelligent overseer (God) to make this happen (the idea that God put particles in motion would gradually disappear in science).

Like Descartes, Newton had no time for mystery which both equated with ignorance and superstition. Newton wanted to purge Christianity of the miraculous. Jesus was not God, or God's son but a man in touch with a higher ideal. The Trinity was an invention to draw pagan converts to Christianity. Nature is the only temple of God.

The Newtonian model of matter was atomistic but not in modern terms. Newton's particles were all thought to be of the same material substance. The differences in matter were the density of atoms packed into any particular matter rather than the difference in the weight and density of the atoms themselves.

Herman Reimarus – Like many in the Age of Reason, he was past looking at Jesus as divine. He promoted Jesus as a man who taught of the peaceful relationship between man and nature. Jesus, according to Reimarus, never got his message across and died in despair. Jesus, Reimarus pointed out never said he came to atone for the sins of mankind. This idea was Paul's invention, the founder of Christianity. Reimarus suggests we do not revere Jesus as God but as a remarkable, simple, exalted and practical teacher.

Francois-Marie de Voltaire – The embodiment of the Enlightenment. While not rejecting the idea of God, he did reject the cruel God of the orthodox, the God that threatened mankind with eternal fire and damnation. He rejected all ideas that were abhorrent to reason. The idea of a God is an invention of man.

Voltaire was quoted as saying "In the beginning God created man in His image, and man promptly returned the favor". The invention of God was the rational thing to do. God is a result of reason not mystery. It all began with a single concept of something out there. From this one something pantheism developed as something more basic to man's comprehension on the earth. Voltaire's problem was not "God" but the doctrine about God, which offended any standard of reason.

Baruch Spinoza – Regarded as one of the first a-theists, he did have a belief in a God but not the God of the Bible. The Israelites called any phenomenon they couldn't understand "God". Inspiration was held to be the domain of the prophets. This Spinoza rejected as a violation of natural reason.

Rituals and symbols are for the masses who are incapable of rational, scientific thought. God is the principal law of nature, the sum of all the eternal laws in existence. God is a material being equal only to the order, which governs the universe.

To speak of God in this world is simply a way of describing the mathematical and causal principal of existence. There is no transcendence, but there is harmony and unity. Like Plato, Spinoza believed that intuitive and spontaneous knowledge reveals the presence of God more than the acquiring of facts. Our joy and happiness in knowledge is equivalent to the love of God. God is not the eternal thought but the cause and principal of that thought which is in every human being.

The Torah is the only eternal law of nature. God is accessible to everyone, all the time. There is nothing personal about God. God is not separate from reality. There can be no separation between the creator (thought) and the created. The proper term is simply "is". God is. The mystics had been saying this for centuries.

Immanuel Kant – The only way to God lies through the autonomous realm of moral conscience, which is called "practical reason". He dismissed dogma, prayer, and ritual, which he believed prevented man from relying on their own powers. To rely on authority for your own power is absurd.

God's existence or non-existence cannot be proved logically, and while logic is the only vehicle of reason why spend all the energy on something that can have no proof. God is simply tacked on to an ethical system as an afterthought.

Diderot – There is no God – only nature. Religion creates gods because humanity couldn't find any other explanation to console them for the tragedy in their lives. Man turns to the imaginary comforts of religion and philosophy in an attempt to establish some illusion of control. Philosophy is not the result of a noble desire for knowledge

(Aristotle), but for the longing to avoid pain. The cradle of religion is ignorance and fear. A mature, enlightened mankind must climb out of religion. God is not merely unnecessary but positively harmful.

By the end of the 17th Century, "atheist" was no longer a disparaging term but a badge of honor among the reformist.

During the 18th and 19th Century one idea after another rose to challenge the traditional view of the Western God. Since Augustine, there was an emphasis on guilt, sin, struggle and strain. Most 18th Century Philosophers were on a mission to get rid of a deity, which caused such widespread lack of confidence for mankind.

Georg Wilhelm Hegel – The Jewish God, the God of the Bible is a tyrant. Christianity fell into the same trap. Judaism is everything that is wrong with religion. Christianity is no better. Reason is superior to religion.

Arthur Schopenhauer – There is no Absolute, no God, and no Spirit at work in the world. There is nothing but brute instinctive will to live. Hinduism and Buddhism had arrived at a just conception of reality when they claimed that everything is *maya* or illusion. People must create a sense of ultimate meaning for themselves therefore they naturally create a God.

There is no need of a savior because there is nothing to be saved from i.e. all is illusion.

Soren Kirkegard – The old creeds and doctrines have become idols, ends in themselves and substitutes for the ineffable reality of God. The idea of God has alienated us from our own nature by posing an impossible perfection next to our human frailty.

Karl Marx – Religion is a sign of the oppressed, the opium of the masses, which makes their suffering bearable. Atheism is as much a waste of time as theism. God is simply irrelevant. There is no meaning, value or purpose outside the historical process. Any idea for or against God has yet to help humanity.

Frederich Nietzche – "God is Dead". The God of the West is a crime against life. This God has encouraged people to fear their bodies, their passions and their sexuality. This God has promoted a morality of compromise, which has made us weak. This God has alienated people from their own humanity and brotherhood.

Sigmund Freud – Belief in God is an illusion for a mature man or woman. The idea of a God to watch over us is a product of the unconscious. A personal god is nothing more than the exalted father figure, which springs from infancy. God is a substitute for this desire. Religion belongs to the infancy of the human race. It was necessary in the beginning just like it is a necessary step from childhood to maturity. Religion is not for the mature, healthy mind. It cannot be abolished however because the psyche still needs the father figure and the fable. It will eventually disappear when humanity grows up.

Carl Jung – God is similar to the God of the mystics. God is not a person, place or thing but a psychological truth, which can be experienced by the individual only in the depths of his subconscious mind. It's there that the symbols of greater understanding can be found. It's the only place.

Today

1. In less than 400 years we have explored our world, founded nations, created a global economy, and sent men to the moon, conquered diseases, developed communication systems that put us in touch with each other instantaneously, and many other amazing accomplishments.

2. The cost have been substantial. We have exploited the natural environment almost to the level of extinction. Since the 17th Century, the materialistic view, while creating greater welfare for the human race, is literally eating itself out of its own home. At the beginning of the 19th Century there were 1 billion humans on planet earth. In 1999 there are 6 billion inhabi-

tants. In 2010 there are over 6.5 billion. By the year 2030 there will be 10 billion!

3. Mankind's focus on the physical world has pushed away some of our anxiety but has reduced life to its economic aspect only. Science set up a worldview that reinforced this obsession and got lost in it. Man is further apart from one another than at any time in history. Ideology seems more important than life itself.

4. The cost of a limited cosmology is the narrowing of human experience and the repression of our higher spiritual perception.

Albert Einstein - His studies shattered the old idea of a mechanical universe. In perhaps his most revolutionary idea, he asserted that the mass of a physical object and the energy it contained were in fact interchangeable. $E = MC2$. In essence, Einstein showed that matter was nothing more than light! Einstein's model forms the basis of quantum mechanics.

The scientific paradigm has now shifted away from the concept of a mechanistic universe. The universe is now being viewed as an organism with total intelligence, direction and purpose. No longer can we think of ourselves as living in a simple world of solid, material stuff. We know that everything around us is a mysterious vibrating pattern of energy; the stuff of light and that includes human beings. We are intimately connected with the universe and with each other. Ultimately there is no separation. Separation is a perception subject to a limited perspective.

Our task now is to recognize this, remember who we are, wake up and go home.

Chapter Three

WHERE GOD COMES FROM

"God" is an ambiguous word in our language because it appears to refer to something that is known. But the transcendent is unknowable and unknown. God is transcendent, finally, of anything like the name "God". God is beyond names and forms. The mystery of life is beyond all human conception. Everything we know is within the terminology of the concepts of being and not being, many and single, true and untrue. We always think in terms of opposites. But God, the ultimate, is beyond the pairs of opposites, that is all there is to it."

Joseph Campbell.

MYTHOLOGY
By: Dr. Joseph Campbell

Hunters

Neolithic man (15,000 BCE) began as a hunter. Man's survival necessitated the hunting, killing and eating of animals. Where today we see the animal as a lower form of life, our ancient ancestors saw the animal as sacred. Ancient myths (stories) given to us in the form of cave art suggests a divine relationship between man and the animal. Early art suggests that, in many ways, the animal was superior to man.

For early man the CAVE (an important symbol throughout all mythology) is the womb of the earth. Out of this womb man emerges to face the terror of his outer world. The cave is both a place where life begins, is protected, and a sanctuary to worship the life giving animal. These caves are our first homes and our first cathedrals. The animal paintings in these caves are not just pictures of animals; they are spiritual images in a deeply spiritual place. The imagery there is beyond the animal, it is in reverence to the life-giving animal. Going there for early man was going into the mystery that brings life. By creating an image of this life-giving animal you were inviting this force into the world to sustain the life of man.

The ritual of going into the earth was a sacred rite of passage for boys. It was an act of becoming a man. From this point on the boy was no longer a boy. He was no longer his mother's son. The boy becomes a man and is identified with his father and is reborn to a greater sense of what he is. By participating in the ritual (which is the enactment of a myth) you are participating in the mystery by which you become a member of your community. You are no longer a child but a man with a greater sense of responsibility.

Geography has done a great deal to shape culture through myth. The God of the desert is not the God of the plains or the rain forest. When you are out in the desert with one sky and one horizon, you might have one deity. In the jungle where there is no horizon, and you never see anything over 20 feet away, you develop many Gods. Very clearly man has projected his idea of God on his world. All gods are an invention of man as a way of answering the question, "where do things come from and a desire that they will return".

Hunter cultures, and the myths that develop from them, are always directed "outward" to the animal. The hunter's life depends on his relationship to the animal. The mythology is outward turned. The animal is "out there", comes from "out there", is always "out there" and if revered will return to sustain man's life.

This is the first development of conscientiousness.

Planters

With the coming of the planting cultures (5,000 BCE.) the mythology, which has to do with cultivation of the plant, the planting of the seed, the death of the seed and the coming of new plants are more "inward". With the hunters, the animals inspired the mythology and the animal became the teacher. In the planter cultures the plant becomes the teacher. The plant world is viewed as being identical in its life sequence with that of man.

As man turned from hunting to planting, there is a dramatic and total transformation, not just of the myths, but also of the psyche itself. When an animal was killed, it's over. Another animal must come from "out there" to replace it.

In the plant world if you cut down a plant another one grows back in its place. The plant returns from almost the same place it left. It comes from "inside" the earth. It comes from mother earth. Thus mythology begins to emphasize the mother as the source of life over the outward animal. The woman's place is elevated in consciousness and gains power in the myths and in the cultural view. The goddess overcomes the god in worship rituals.

In the planter cultures, there is a sense that death is not death, but a brief transition and is required for new life. The individual is no longer an individual but a branch of the plant, a part of the whole. Life is a cycle: birth, death, and resurrection.

The death and resurrection of the plant is the death and resurrection of the savior myth. The birth, death and resurrection of a savior figure run through planter cultures worldwide. Across the planet we can find stories where someone dies, is buried and out of his body comes the life giving plant. Someone had to die in order for life to emerge. This is a common mythic form. It is the basis of the Christian myth.

In the Christian tradition, when Christ is crucified, it's from his body that the food of spirit comes. The Christ story comes to us from a very solid planter culture myth. Jesus on the tree is the fruit of the tree.

Jesus is the fruit of eternal life, which is the fruit of the second tree in the Garden of Eden, "The Tree of Life". Getting back into the Garden is the motif of many a religion. In the Christian myth, eating the fruit of Jesus brings you back to the Garden. This is the basis of Catholic communion.

In planter cultures there is a notion that you die to the vehicle (the body) and become identified with that which the vehicle is the carrier (the essence), the one radiance which shines through all things. The translation of that to the person becomes: I die to my flesh and am born into spirit. My body is a vehicle, which gives way to the carrier – God. Death is never rejected in the myths. Death is not an opposite to life but two aspects of the same thing, of being and becoming.

What the myths are attempting to do is teach you how to penetrate the labyrinth of life in such a way that its spiritual values come through. You are always in transition toward a larger way of living. You die to your little self to be reborn to your larger Self. You are that which is a "part" and the "all" at the same instant.

The myths that subsequent cultures go on to develop have both hunter and planter culture myths connected to them. The Greeks can be said to have practically institutionalized mythology. Everything the Greeks did was based on an elaborate creation of gods and goddesses and their interaction with man.

What is Mythology?

Before the advent of science (17th Century), superstitions, legends and folklore defined the world, man, God and the relationships between the three. This is a world of church directed mythology. The unknown was a frightening place. Better to put a face on it than nothing at all. And of course the church was the authority.

With the development of science ("The Age of Enlightenment", sometimes called the "Age of Reason"), rational thinking would take the place of the myths. Indeed science did dispel much of the belief system that was held in place for 1,000 years by an ignorant priesthood. For more than 1,000 years man was to believe that the earth was the center of the solar system and the heavens were a canopy over the earth. The stars were holes in the canopy through which the gods watched us, etc.

Through the 20th century, science has indeed given us a "rational" model for understanding our physical world. For the last 400 years we have relied on that Newtonian, Cartesian Principle, of "cause and effect". Recently however, Quantum (non linear) physics has come along to say that nothing is "absolutely" verifiable. The "rational" has suddenly become irrational. There be no beginning and no end. There's no such thing as mass. Everything is an expression of light. There's only light in one form or another. Everything is in transition. Nothing is permanent or final. The new science is beginning to say what the ancients said – There only is!

Mythology's Basic Theme

There is an invisible or "apparent" plane supporting the visible plane. The approach to understanding these two perceptions is either subjective (metaphysical) or objective (physical).

A Myth is simply a story

The word comes from the Greek word "*mythos*" which means story. However, all stories are not myths.

Myths are stories about gods and goddesses and man's relationship to them. Myths are stories that attempt to explain universal truths.

Myths are the stories that inform a society about who they are.

Myths validate the social order, such as "rule by divine right", which is still the dominating view of the competing world.

Because myths are stories about gods and goddesses and man's relationship thereto, myths become the basis for religion. Seen another way, religion is what happens in an attempt to interpret the myths.

Religion is what results from misunderstanding the myths. Religion is therefore the great misunderstanding. Religions get stuck on the story rather than the meaning of the story.

Myths fill a void that science can't resolve. Man's eternal questioning of: Who am I? Why am I here? What's the meaning of life? Is there a God? If so, where is He? etc. These questions cannot be answered by science alone. Science can only give us a physical (linear) answer, which is now in question.

What about the metaphysical answer? That's why we have mythology. Mythology deals with the metaphysical, the place where science cannot go. Mythology looks at the abstract. Science looks at measurement.

Legends are not myths. Legends may or may not have historical accuracy, but there is usually an element of truth in a legend. e.g. King Arthur, Camelot and the Knights of the Round Table. The question in legends are, were they stories or metaphors? Are they real or a legend or a piece of both?

Folktales are not myths but are stories that entertain or instruct society. These are adventurous stories about heroes and magical happenings. e.g. the search for the Holy Grail or the golden flees. Myths have elements of legends and folktales in them and vice versa.

Myths are stories, which beg to be told. Indeed language itself developed as a human need to tell a story. Until writing was developed humans could only "tell" their story. The oral tradition was the only tradition there was up to the 16th Century. The masses have been held to their oral traditions for most of recorded history (5,000 years). Oral traditions still exist today in primitive cultures.

Art was the first tradition before the oral. The artists in all traditions are the "seers" who inform the society of the meaning of life through the artist's eyes. Belief systems often follow the artist's insight. This has been true in all ages of mankind. To understand a cultures mythology, look at their art. Besides art many oral traditions developed poetry and song because it was easier to remember their story and repeat it word for word.

About Myths

1. Myths define social customs and beliefs.
2. Myths are the same as rituals.
3. Myths are allegories (symbols).
4. Myths explain natural phenomena.
5. Myths explain psychological phenomena such as love, sex and anger toward ones parents. (Sigmund Freud)
6. Myths contain archetypes (elementary or grounding ideas) that reveal the collective unconscious of the human race. (Carl Jung)
7. Myths are a way of communicating and helping people work together or talk about things that cause anxiety.

Major Categories

1. Creation Myths – Where did the world and its creatures come from?
2. Cosmology – How is the land, sea, sky and underworld put together and what is the sun and moon and stars and how do they work together?
3. Origin of Man – Who are we? Where did we come from?
4. Flood Stories – Why did God destroy his creation?
5. Disease and Death – A result of the "fall" of man.
6. Afterlife – What happens to the soul? Is there a soul?

7. Supernatural Beings – Some are good and some are evil. Why both?

8. Dawn of Civilization – Man coming to live apart from the animals with the help and direction of the gods.

9. Foundation Myths – The justification for founding empires. Like manifest destiny.

Myths have a cast of characters, which are fairly standard in all cultures. There are divine deities or gods and the humans who interact with them. Extra special humans get to be heroes. Usually the myths cast a variety of magical animals and tricksters whose whole purpose is to stir up things.

Joseph Campbell defines Mythology as an organization of symbolic images and narratives.

The language of the myths is "metaphor"(something that takes the place of a complex idea). The myth could be an object, an expression, an idea or a symbol. Because some concepts are too difficult to be expressed without long discussion, society has adopted an agreed upon system of metaphors to define things quickly. Mostly our understanding is metaphysical not physical.

Over one half the people in the world believes that the "metaphor" of their religious tradition is factual and literal. These people are called "theists". The other half contends they are not facts at all but metaphor. These people are classified as "a-theists" meaning without theology, rules or dogma.

Metaphors only seem to describe the outer world of time and space. Their real universe is the spiritual universe of the inner life. How can the literalist say "The Kingdom of God is within you" as did the Gnostics and claim everything in the "word" is literal. This is not a linear or literal statement. It is obviously metaphorical and beyond the scope of religion. The statement belongs to mythology not religion.

To understand metaphors one need to understand two terms:

Connotative – That which is implied by a word. (Subjective-Metaphysical- Metaphorical, Abstract)

Denotative – That which is assumed by a word. (Objective-Physical-Factual-Measurable)

Example:

The "Virgin Birth" or "End of the World" or "The Promised Land" or "The Chosen People" taken denotatively, makes these events actual and physical.

Taken connotatively suggest there are conceptual ideas, possibly abstract, beyond the mundane or obvious.

Judeo – Christian – Islamic mythology rests on the denotative interpretation rather than on the connotative. Their teachings are that the symbols are facts not metaphors. This is their great misunderstanding.

Western Traditions (West of Iran including the Near East and Europe. This would include Zoroastrianism, Judaism, Christianity and Islam). In all of these religions (creeds) God made the world and God and the World are not the same. There is no identity with God. God and man are separate. However man can develop a relationship with God as long as man is submissive to God.

All these religions are male dominated. This God marks the domination of the Goddess, which preceded it from the Planter Cultures.

In the West, the divine is not "in" mankind as it is in the East. The Bible tells us that nature is corrupt and that man fell from the grace of God and is a sinner. Man is a sinner because man can't live up to laws that man made for himself! In this tradition you can only know God through an institution. God is outside of mankind. God is in the "rules."

Eastern Tradition

East of Iran, which includes India and the Far East. There is no mythology of God separate from man. Each human is believed to be a part of God. Each individual is divine or an extension of the divine in the physical world. We are God having a human experience. The experience is neither good nor bad, it's our personal experience governed by "karma". In the West we are emptied of our divinity. It is turned over to a social organization.

The primary purpose of a dynamic mythology is to awaken and maintain in the individual a sense of awe, a sense of humility and respect of that ultimate mystery that transcends every name and form. The experience of mystery comes not from expecting it but through yielding your programs to it. Programs are based on desire and fear (the two angels at the exit to the Garden of Eden). The way back into the garden is to conquer desire and fear.

Notions of God

God is not a fact. A fact is an object in the field of time and space, an image in the dream field. God is no dream, no fact. God is a word that refers us past anything we can conceive of or name. God for most people has sentiments much like they do, liking certain people better than others and having certain rules for their lives. "God" is mostly a reflection of His creator.

In almost all other belief systems, other than Western, gods are agents or imagined functionaries that transcend all conceptualization. God, in these beliefs, is not the source of energy but the agent of energy. God is informing reality not reality itself. In other words, what you see in the world is where God has been, not where God is. God is the residual effect of that energy.

Myths like dreams are products of the imagination.

1. **Simple, personal dreams.** The dreamer becomes involved in adventures reflective of the dreamers own personal problems, the conflicts of his life between desires and fears, driving wishes and moral prohibitions.

2. **Visions.** Where one transcends the sphere of a personal horizon and comes into confrontation with the same great "universal" problems that are symbolized in all-great myths.

Just think about it. We have come forth from this Earth of ours. The Earth came forth from our galaxy and the galaxy from the condensation of atoms gathered from space. The Earth is a precipitate of space. Humans are the precipitates of Earth, the sensory organs of the Earth and the Universe. We have it all right within us. The deities we thought were "out there", we now know are projections. They are the products of our own imaginations. They were an attempt to define and interpret the mysteries of the Universe.

Indeed it is a very different Universe today from the days of the Jewish God YAHWEH that threw down stones on the Amorites and caused the sun to stand still in the sky until his "chosen Nation" took revenge on its enemies. (Joshua 10:13) Most of the Jewish Gods, and there were many following the Egyptian tradition, were war gods including Jehovah who ultimately survived his competitors by the time of Moses.

From <u>Origin of the Idea of God</u> by Father Wilhelm Schmidt – 1912:

"In the beginning human beings created a God who was "first cause" of all things and the ruler of heaven and earth. This God was not represented by images, had no temple erected to him or priests in his service. He was too exalted for an inadequate human cult. Gradually he faded from human consciousness. He had become so remote that the people decided they didn't need him anymore. Eventually he disappeared."

Mythologies are directly proportional to Consciousness. "When I was a child, I spoke as a child. When I became a man I put away childish things." We have held to an ancient, parochial mythology long enough. God is not dead. But indeed He has disappeared. He waits in the wings of our awakening.

About 14,000 years ago our modern God idea begins to take root in the Middle East. These early humans felt they were surrounded by the unseen. To resolve this problem they began putting a face on the unseen so they could see it. The god idea begins.

Primitive monotheism existed prior to pantheism. The "sky God" is one of the earliest ideas coming out of Africa. This God was not personal. This God was just there, watching over things. Gradually losing consciousness of this distant high god, man begins to replace him with more attractive and available gods. Monotheism is an original and impersonal idea developed by primitive man to explain the mystery and tragedy of life. Creating gods is something that humans have always done. If one idea ceases to work, just replace it with another.

When man began to create god and the myths to go along with this deity, they were not seeking a literal explanation for natural phenomena. They were expressing their wonder and trying to link that wonder to their lives. Myths are not to be taken literally, but are metaphorical attempts to describe the indescribable. People needed a way to articulate their sense of the powerful but unseen forces around them.

The ancients believed that by participating in the divine, they would become truly human. Everything on Earth was believed to a replica of something in the divine world. Participation in life brought man and god together. Does this sound like "The Kingdom of God is spread out upon the earth. The Kingdom of God is where you are."

Religion

The problem for and the function of religion in our age is to awaken the heart. This is only possible if the clergy are able to interpret the symbols through an expanded awareness. To the degree the priesthood can bring the connotative message rather than the denotative message rests the future of religion. Religion will not survive unless it grows up. A new mythology will have to be developed and accepted. Quite possibly the new mythology will be part ancient myth and new science. In any event the current Judeo Christian myth has run its course. It is no longer believable.

Symbols of the Judeo-Christian Tradition:

Genesis

Borrowed from the Sumerian Civilization 3300 – 1900 BCE. Approximately 2,000 years before Moses and the Torah.

The first part of the story is sheer mythology and that of the Mesopotamian people. The "Garden of Eden" is a mythological place in a mythological age. The story of "not eating the apple of the forbidden tree" is an old folklore tale that is called the "one forbidden thing".

There is always something in these stories that man is not to do. Do not open this door, do not look over there, do not eat this food etc.

So what about this garden? It was a place of unity, of oneness, of no division in the nature of people or things. Eating of the fruit of the "Tree of Knowledge of Good and Evil" allows for the knowledge of the pairs of opposites: good and evil, light and dark, right and wrong, male and female, and God and man. The fruit, once eaten puts man out of the Garden (Unity) and the gate is closed and guarded by 2 cherubim. (Fear and Desire) There is no longer a sense of oneness. There is only a sense of separation.

So, how do we get back into this Garden? By eating from the "Tree of Life". What does this mean? The way back is the way out. One must live on two levels: Living out of the recognition of life as it is without judgment and by living in terms of the ethical values of one's culture or one's particular personal religion.

God did not exile Adam and Eve. They exiled themselves. The Garden is a metaphor for our minds and our thinking in terms of opposites. The two cherubim that guard the gate back to oneness are Fear and Desire: the fear of death and the desire for more of this world. The way back into the Garden is overcoming fear and desire. Removing the cherubim will allow you to see that everything is "One". This is a psychological, spiritual experience.

The Kingdom of Heaven is where you are and the way there is through Forgiveness. Not forgiveness in a moral sense but in the sense that you are "willing" to see the error of accepting duality as real. Forgiveness is going beyond the illusion of separation to a greater awareness of oneness or connection. This is the trip "in" not the trip "out."

This our ancient forefathers understood but we have forgotten. In our "remembering" we reenter the Garden.

The Jews think of themselves as in exile. A word very much their own. They have thrown themselves out of the Garden and have been thrown out of their county on various occasions. The central theme of the Old Testament is that of exile. Christianity, through Jesus, found a way out of exile. Christ, in the New Testament, represents a reentry into the Garden.

By following the message of forgiveness we find that the "Kingdom" is here on the Earth, where we are. Salvation is man "awakening" to this reality. The misunderstanding in the myth of Jesus is that Jesus will do it for us. The hero brings the message only. He is not the message, which is often confused by the observer. A change in view (repentance) is always up to the people.

The Virgin Birth

This myth occurs in the lives of great and not so great persons in mythology.

Greek – Deities propagate sons from nymphs thus creating sons of gods. The female is always a virgin.

Celtic – The warrior/hero goes off to battle. Before leaving the warrior begets a son. The hero dies, the son is born and the mother is called a virgin.

Buddha – While his birth was not held as miraculous, his mother was called a virgin.

India – Vyasa, the "Homer" of India was a result of a virgin birth.

The Catholic Church emphasizes the historical, physical (denotative) character of the virgin birth by saying that Mary's virginity was in place before the birth and was restored to her after the birth. This is an "article of faith" and is not to be questioned. This is a failure to understand the myth.

The Gnostics believed that the virgin birth of Christ in the womb of Mary was not to be understood as a literal event but rather the birth of divine Wisdom in the soul. The virgin birth is a metaphor for something wonderful. This is a connotative idea not denotative.

The Hebrew word for virgin is *almah*, which means a young woman. In the later Greek translation *almah* was changed to *neanis*, which mean virgin. To the Greeks the Son of God must surely come from a virgin not simply a young woman. The Church knew this was a mistranslation but left it in. This is how it has come down to us today.

Go back far enough and you find that every one of the ancient races had a planetary Mother whose fatherless Son became the Savior of the world. From these virgin earth mothers it was only a step to virgin human mothers, overshadowed by a deity whose semi-divine son became a miracle worker.

The Cave

The motif of birth in a cave is very ancient. The mythological Jesus is born in a cave where all other Saviors are born. This cave was always in a wilderness of some kind. In Latin countries, the nativity is still portrayed in a cave, called a *"creche"*.

On December 25th the Persians celebrated the birth of their Savior, Zoroaster in a cave and called him "the Ram of God who takes away the sins of the world." This cave was a manger or horse stall. (Sound familiar?)

The animals are likewise mythological. The ass, at that time was the symbolic animal of Set (darkness) and the ox was the symbolic animal of Osiris (light). These symbols are present in the Sumerian Civilization even prior to the Egyptian civilization. The two powers of light and dark are united in the savior figure. The mythology translates that both light and darkness are recognizing Christ for who He is. Because this representation was ancient it could not be mistaken and was therefore adapted. The Jewish prophets knew this.

No one knows when Jesus was born or where. December 25th was not set for his birth until the 4th Century CE. This of course is in the dead of winter and shepherds do not tend their flocks in the dead of winter and not at night! December 25th was a Roman pagan holiday. It was also the winter solstice, a time when spiritual forces are most active. Physical nature is asleep. The mystics believed that "as the night time is the daytime of the soul, so winter is the daytime of the soul. Winter is the time of spiritual attainment. Failure to understand the mythology leads to false assumptions.

Bethlehem

Why Bethlehem? Was it to fulfill a prophecy or a tax decree? Neither. Jesus was reported born in Bethlehem for the same reasons Joseph and David were born there: Bethlehem is the mystic "house of bread". Jesus was most likely born in Nazareth.

The Star

Again, we have a metaphor. Had such a phenomenon actually occurred two thousand years ago, would someone have not recorded it? Even the great Ptolemy never mentioned it because it never happened. The mystic translation: out of the womb of time and space a sun is born. It was an easy step to "son" is born by the Israelite prophets.

Saturn, the closest and largest planet at that time is also the main star in the constellation Pisces, the star and constellation of Israel!

The Magi and Gifts

The Magi have been showing up for Centuries. They came from the East to offer gold, frankincense and myrrh at the birth of Socrates. At the birth of Krishna (1200 BCE) angels and prophets attended the birth bringing gifts of gold, frankincense and myrrh. When Confucius was born (598 BCE) five wise men came. Celestial music was heard and angels were seen in the skies. Magi also attended the births of Mithra, Zoroaster and Osiris and of course there were angels and music.

Magi, gold, frankincense and myrrh, angles, shepherds and celestial music are all standard mythic equipment.

The Messiah

The idea of a Messiah was an adaptation of the Hebrews from the Persians. When they were in exile in Babylon the Jews invented a Messiah to come and liberate them and reestablish Israel as a nation. This messiah idea was copied from the life of Zoroaster or Zarathustra. John the Baptist is said to have recognized that Jesus was the Messiah. It was at this point that Mary becomes a goddess, the woman who delivered the Messiah.

After going to John, who by the way may have been Jesus cousin, Jesus heads for the desert for 40 days and nights. This parallels the Buddha who after studying with a master goes on his journey. Both undergo three great temptations. Both return to the world to present a great teaching. This is the basic mythic theme of the hero. The hero goes away and returns with a great revelation or truth.

Miracles

Many of the miracles Jesus was said to have performed were borrowed from previous Hebrew writings. Elisha and Elijah both walked on water. Healing the sick and raising the dead are all old myths. The Buddha walked on water. Miracle working is always a sign of divinity in the myths. There never was an age of miracles or miracle workers. Like Saviors these things belong to mythology. St. Augustine tells us he only accepted Christianity because of the overwhelming evidence of the miracles. There are no miracles here but there are morals. The stories around Jesus doing miracles are misinterpreted myths regarding morality.

The Crucifixion

There were 16 Saviors crucified on a cross prior to Jesus. The cross is not a Christian origination. It is a universal symbol found on temples, tablets and artifacts throughout the ancient world. The significance of the cross is not due to the fact that Saviors were crucified on it. They were crucified on it because of the cross's significance.

The original Christian symbol was the swastika. Which was the symbol of creative motion. The word is Sanskrit, which means, "It is well." The early Christians wore the symbol as a statement of good cheer. Later a lamb was used for Aries then a fish for Pisces etc. The crucifix was substituted about 400 years after the mythic crucifixion.

The Christian myth is that Jesus died for our sins. That was the sacrificial message borrowed from the Jews in the "scape goat" idea. We still believe that God, in his infinite love, sacrificed his Son to save us from perdition. This we call "vicarious atonement", but for what? Did man commit the original sin or did God commit it? St. Anselm wrote in the Middle Ages that, "Christ came not to save man from the condemnation of God, but to save God from the condemnation of man." Having made a world of pain and suffering, God needed exoneration, and sent his representative to plead God's case before mankind. This is the love and mercy teaching of his dutiful Son, who died to save his Father from the growing suspicion of pagan enlightenment.

In any event it's all mythology. The meanings are all much, much deeper.

After Jesus death, his followers decided He must have been divine. Jesus as the Son of God was not finalized in creed until the 4th century C.E. Paul, the founder of Christianity, never claimed that Jesus was God or the Son of God. This would have been against the Jewish law. The confusion comes because the old Jewish prophecy forecast a Messiah to save the Jews from exile. People wanting to believe that Jesus was the Messiah began to attach an even higher accolade upon the man. Messiah, Savior, and then Devine. This is the order of the myth.

Paul tells us that Jesus referred to himself as the son of man, which comes from the Aramaic phrase *(barnasha)*, which means the weakness and mortality of the human condition. If Jesus said this, he saw himself as a frail human being who would one day suffer and die. Is this a statement that the living Son of God would make?

Miracles, according to Paul, comes from the Aramaic *(dunamix)* which means powers. Jesus tried to make it clear that we all have these healing powers. There were many "healers" wandering the countryside. It was the only form of healing there was. Any healing was held to be a miracle by the people. Anything not understandable was a miracle. All desert healers were performing miracles. Most illnesses were psychosomatic to begin with.

The New Testament is primarily a number of letters written by Paul of Tarsus to answer questions from the Roman provinces. Paul never intended that his reflections would become a full-blown theology. This came 320 years later at the Council of Nicea at the direction of Constantine to solve a conflict between the Church of Rome and the Church of Constanople. The idea that Jesus died for our sins (the atonement) was never theology until the 4th Century. That Jesus died to atone for Adam's sin never surfaced until the Council put it in the creed. Even then it was not important in the East, only in the West.

During the 1st Century, Christians (calling themselves The Way) continued to think about God much the same as their Jewish brothers. Their "churches" were the same as synagogues. In 80 C.E., The Way was no longer allowed in Jewish synagogues because the followers of Jesus refused to observe the teachings of the Torah.

The Romans never saw a difference between The Way and the Jewish belief system. They saw this new sect as a branch of Judaism. Once the Jews put the followers of Jesus out of the synagogue, the Romans began looking at them as fanatics for breaking with tradition. Any break with the past was viewed as heresy and punished by death.

In the Roman Empire no one expected the idea of religion to provide an answer to the meaning of life. This was the domain of the philosophers, who were mainly the Greek philosophers (pagans) who the Romans revered. The Romans worshiped the gods mainly to ask for help during a crisis or to secure a blessing for the state. Romans tolerated all beliefs as a means of continuity with the past.

This is not too far removed from our own perception today. Our system tolerates most anything as long as it doesn't create grief for the governing body. As long as the belief is not too exotic or promotes drastic change, it is tolerated. People don't expect brilliant new ideas from sermons and are in fact upset by them. People want ritual to be consistent and get upset if changes occur in procedure. This is the portrait of the pagan worshiper in the 1st Century Rome. Is it still the portrait of the 21st Century worshiper?

Educated pagans looked to philosophy not religion for enlightenment. Conversion to Christianity in the pagan world didn't begin until the end of the 2nd Century. This conversion adopted Greco-Roman ideals.

Clement of Alexandria (150-215 C.E.) was an early convert who had an impact on "Christian" thinking. He wrote that man could participate in the "divine life" by imitating the calmness of God. "A Christian should be serene: sit correctly, speak quietly, refrain from violent, convulsive laughter and burp gently." This was Clement's perception of becoming quiet within. If Jesus were God and preached gentleness, then the imitation of Jesus would bring on divinity.

Origen, Clement's pupil, (known for his self castration) emphasized turning against the world. He believed that martyrdom was a straight path to God. His family had been martyred. Origen like Clement adopted Plato's belief that man had a soul. This soul continues its upward assent to God in a long steady journey even after death. By contemplating God the soul ultimately becomes divine and going to God. Belief in Jesus the man was only a phase. Jesus was here to help us on our way, but it is entirely up to us if we want to become divine.

In the 9th Century (Dark Ages) the church condemned Origen and Clement mainly because neither of them supported the idea that God made the world out of nothing, which was becoming church doctrine. Neither believed that man was saved by the death and resurrection of Jesus. They in fact believed and taught that man gets to heaven by his own choices.

<u>Plotinus</u> (205-270 C.E.)

Studied under Clement's teacher, Saccus, in Alexandria. While visiting Antioch and listening to the teachings of Paul, he came to believe that the teaching was a thoroughly objectionable creed.

Drawing on Plato's idea, Plotinus evolved a system designed for the individual to achieve an understanding of the self. His ideas would influence all three of the great religions. Instead of looking to the physical world, he urged his students to go within to the depths of the psyche (soul). Ultimate reality was primal unity, which he called the "One". All reality owes their existence to this single theme.

The "One" is simplicity itself. It just is. It is nameless. It is not a thing but distinct from all things. It is everything and nothing at the same time. The "One" must have transcended itself, gone beyond its simplicity in order to make itself understood to imperfect beings like us. As in the Gnostic myths, the further a being gets from its source in the "One", the weaker it becomes.

All beings yearn for unity. They long to return to the "One". This is not a journey toward but a journey into the depths of being, the depths of mind. The soul, in these depths, will remember the simplicity it has forgotten and return to its true self. The "One" is impersonal. It has no gender and is entirely oblivious of us.

Plotinus's philosophy was not a logical process but a spiritual quest. A quest where we do not cling to God but to a state of mind where we see God and ourselves as light itself, pure, buoyant, aerial.

The notion of an enlightenment that is impersonal, natural and beyond human category is pure Buddhism. This was attractive to may early Christians as a statement of their own personal experience.

Eastern Roman Empire

By 235 C.E., Christianity was making big strides. In 312 C.E., Constantine, following a vision and wining a great battle and at the insistence of his mother, declared Christianity the official religion of Rome in 313 C.E. Paganism still flourished for another 200 years. Roman approval of Christianity sealed its victory. Now comes the problem of conformity.

The first problem between East and West was the issue of the Trinity. Constantine summoned all the church heads to a meeting in Nicea, Turkey (May 20, 325) out of which we get the first Creed – The Nicene Creed which established what the church believed in...We believe in.... and the last line stated "And we believe in the Holy Spirit" to appeal to the pagans. Thus the Trinity was in the East. In the West there was still resistance. But no one was to go up against the emperor.

Western Roman Empire

Augustine is called the founder of the Western spirit. Other than Paul, no one had a bigger impact on belief. Augustine sought for a theistic religion. He did not see Christianity as incompatible with Plato or Plotinus. He saw God as essential to humanity. God is both in man and above man. This is a paradox and is again Buddhism. The twist for Augustine was that God is not impersonal but very personal like in the Jewish tradition. He believed that man was damned and only by grace would he be allowed into heaven. The guilt of being a descendant of Adam came out in the sexual act. During sex we are no longer rational and while swamped with passion God is forgotten. Therefore, there can be no sex for those wanting to know God.

Our heritage from Augustine is that we are flawed, especially the female. "Women are an evil influence on man, a temptress and a danger to mankind." "Whether it is a wife or a mother, it is still Eve the temptress that we must be aware of." Western Christianity never fully recovered from this neurotic male prejudice.

Justinian and Theodora (529 CE.)

These Roman rulers closed the ancient school of philosophy in Athens, which was the last bastion of intellectual paganism in the world. The Dark Ages had just begun. The Greek view brought Christianity closer to the oriental tradition. Justinian forever set the course of Christianity on a Western path, a path of dogma and darkness for over 1,000 years.

Council of Trent – England (1545 CE.)

Sets up the Catholic and Protestant dogma we have today.

Chapter Four

THE GNOSTICS

The Jesus Mysteries
By Timothy Freke &
Peter Gandy

In 1945, in a cave near Nag Hammadi, Egypt, an entire Gnostic library was found. It would revolutionize our understanding of the early Gnostics. Up until this time the Literalist Christian Church had given us the only definition we had of Gnosticism and it wasn't pretty. Gnostics were attacked and physically hounded out of existence by the Church. Gnostics were referred to as Pagans, the very definition of which was a distortion of the facts.

"Pagan" as defined by the Church meant "country dweller". The denotation was that the spirituality of the ancients was primitive superstition and was followed by ignorant, rural people.

Of course the Pagans built the Pyramids and the Parthenon. Sculptured Phideus. Pagans wrote the plays of Euripides and Sophocles. Pagans numbered the great philosophers such as Plato and Socrates and the great mathematicians of Pythagoras and Aristotle. The Pagans built the Library of Alexandria housing hundreds of thousands of scrolls on every subject known to man. Pagans had authored great advancements in biology, astronomy and law. Pagans gave us Democracy, rational philosophy, theater and the Olympic games.

In other words Pagans gave us a blueprint for a modern world.

Country people did practice nature worship to maintain the fertility of the land. As in every other part of the world, people found themselves close to the worship practices of their ancestors.

There was another group of Pagans – "the thinkers". They practiced religions known as "The Mysteries". The rites of the Mysteries are called "initiations" – an individualistic form of spirituality, which offered mystical vision and personal enlightenment.

At the heart of Pagan philosophy, whether country dweller or cosmopolitan was the understanding that all things were ONE! The Mysteries aimed at awakening within the initiate a sublime experience of this ONENESS!

Plotinus, the most influential philosopher after Plato, describes the initiate transcending his limited sense of himself as a separate ego and experiencing mystical union with God. Plotinus studied at the great Gnostic library of Alexandria for eleven years under the great Gnostic sage Saccus. In Rome, Emperors and senators attended Saccus's lectures.

The Pagan Mystery religions were practiced for thousands of years throughout the ancient world. The central theme revolved around a dying and resurrecting godman. The godman myth was that of dying to the lower animal nature to be reborn into the higher Christ consciousness. Greek Gnosticism called this lower animal nature the "eidolon"(false self), the embodied self, the physical body, the personality. The higher consciousness the "daemon", the Spirit, the true self, the immortal self, each person's connection to God. The goal of Gnostic initiation was to bring the lower self into union with the Higher Self thus achieving enlightenment.

In one of the Gnostic Gospel's found at Nag Hammadi the risen Jesus calls the Literalist Christianity an "imitation church", an attempt to take the place of the true Christian brotherhood of the Gnostics. From the Gnostic point of view it was the literalists who had distorted Christianity, not the other way around. To the Gnostics, literal Christianity preached only the outer mysteries, which they called a "worldly

Christianity" suitable for "people in a hurry." These comments aren't from some little known heretic but from the writings of none other than Origen and Clement, the heads of the first Christian philosophical school at Alexandria. The Catholic Church later sainted Clement.

Gnosticism was a broad, vibrant and sophisticated spirituality, which was attractive to the greatest Christian intellectuals of the first few Centuries CE. Although Pagan sages talked about gods and goddesses, they maintained a completely mystical and transcendent understanding of the supreme God.

The supreme God of the Pagan Mysteries was an ineffable Oneness beyond all qualities, which could not be described in words. The Gnostics also adopted this abstract and mystical conception of God. God wasn't some big guy in the sky, but was understood as the Mind of the Universe, which expresses itself through all beings.

Jehovah, the god of the Jews, was seen as a partisan, capricious and sometimes tyrannical tribal deity. Jehovah was pictured by the Gnostics as a presumptuous lesser deity who ignorantly believed Himself to be the one true God. "I am a jealous god, and there is no other gods but me." The Gnostics observed, who was there to be jealous of if Jehovah was the only god?

Plato argued that belief is concerned only with the "appearance of things" while knowledge penetrates to the underlying reality. The highest level of understanding is that through knowledge, the mind becomes unified with the object of knowledge. "I and the Father are one" is such an understanding.

Gnostics inherited these Pagan teachings and were dubious of *pistis* (faith) in comparison with *Gnosis* (knowledge). Gnosis is a mystical "experience" of truth which is immediate, certain, and completely non-conceptual. Literalist Christianity promoted "blind faith" and commanded the faithful not to question. Literalists promoted ignorance of anything not literal.

The Alexandrian poet, Valentinus, wrote that a person receives Gnosis from their Guardian Angel which in reality is the seeker's own Higher Self (Daemon). When the human self (eidolon) and the divine "I" (Daemon) are interconnected perfection is achieved. Once enlightened the initiate discovers that actually there is only one Daemon shared by all – a universal Self, which inhabits every being. Each soul is a part of the one Soul of God.

The famous Gnostic inscription above the doorway leading into Gnostic temples – Gnothi Seauton –means "Know Thyself" or "In knowing oneself one knows God" or "Man Know Thy Self As God". The Daemon is actually the one soul of the Universe. When we discover who we are, we discover that there is only God.

Reincarnation

In the Pagan/Gnostic Mysteries it was believed that a soul progressed toward the realization of Gnosis over many lifetimes. The unenlightened soul is attracted back into physical incarnation over and over again by the force of habit. Plutarch, a prolific author, philosopher and Priest of Apollo at Delphi for the last 30 years of his life wrote, "A soul will continue to reincarnate until it is eventually saved from its lack of perception, attains Gnosis, and so is perfected, after which it no longer goes into another flesh."

The Pistis Sophia (Goddess of Wisdom) teaches that a soul cannot be brought into the Light until, through many lifetimes of experience, it has understood all of the mysteries. Each lifetime is the great opportunity for Gnosis, without which the initiate cannot go on.

Plato tells us that the dead have the choice of drinking from the "Spring of Memory" and walking the right-hand path toward heaven or from the "Cup of Forgetting" and walking the left-handed path toward reincarnation. Plato saw being incarnated in a human body as comparable to being incarcerated in a sort of prison. "The soul is suffering the self imposed penalty for the making of bad choices until the penalty is paid."

Pagan/Gnostics didn't believe that a just and compassionate God would condemn any soul to an eternity of hell, but thought that all souls would be saved through experiencing repeated human incarnations. Origen, an early Christian Literalist turned Gnostic writes, "Every soul has existed from the beginning. It has therefore passed through some worlds already, and will pass through others before it reaches the final consummation. It comes into the world strengthened by its victories or weakened by its defeats of the previous life. By the way Origen was posthumously condemned as a heretic by the Roman Catholic Church in the 5th Century and ordered that all his writings be burned.

The Gnostic Christians did not regard their gospels as historical records but works of allegorical literature encoding eternal truths that could be creatively developed and refined. It was only through direct personal contact with the "Living One" that one determines what is true not second-hand testimony or tradition.

The Pagan satirist Celsus wrote of Christian literalism in the first century:

1. God creates a garden for man then banishes him from it.

2. The world is created in "days" before "days" were created, without heavens or a sun. How could the concept of "days" exist without a sun or sky?

3. The Christian literal God wears himself out and must rest on the seventh day!

Celsus concludes, "A God who gets tired, works with his hands, and gives orders like a foreman is not acting very much like a God". This was viewed as simple-minded and superficial. How could anyone not see these stories were clearly allegorical? Do you think Celsus would be shocked to hear modern fundamentalists saying the same thing 2,000 years later?

The Christian Church has failed to understand, for 2,000 years, that what is taken to be literal statements and events are in fact carefully constructed mystical allegories. With the destruction of the Inner Mysteries of the Gnostics, the keys to decode the allegories have been lost and we can only guess at much of the profound metaphor at work in the Jesus story.

Daemon – Eidolon

For Gnostics, the godman Jesus symbolized the Daemon (the immortal self). The Eidolon (the incarnate self) refers to the lower animal self or consciousness and in the Gospel of Thomas is called Jesus "twin brother".

The purpose of Gnostic initiation was to free initiates from all suffering through the realization that their true identity is not the eidolon, bound to the cross of matter, but the Daemon that witnesses life as a passing illusion. A great Gnostic truth: "what one resists – persists. What one looks at disappears". This is the definition of apparent reality- the illusion.

According to the Pagan sages, we are each made up of a mortal eidolon and an immortal Daemon. If we are alive to our personal identity as the eidolon, we are dead to our eternal identity as the Daemon.

Initiation in the Mysteries was a way to bring the soul back to life. By undergoing a mystical death of the eidolon the initiate could arise reborn as the Daemon. This death/resurrection concept was in practice for a thousand years before the literalist attempted to make it unique and historical in Jesus.

Literalist Christians rested their faith entirely on the supposed miracle that a historical Jesus had physically come back from the dead and that this was some sort of proof that those who believed that Jesus was the "Son of God" would also be resurrected physically at the "Day of Judgment". The Gnostics, in contrast, called taking the resurrection literally the "faith of fools!"

Resurrection to the Gnostics could happen to any of us right here and now through the recognition of our true identity as the daemon not the eidolon. Resurrection was simply "the revealing of what truly exists". The resurrection was simply a change in awareness, a waking up to the fact that the daemon has already taken place. In fact the individual's daemon was the universal daemon, which the Gnostics pictured as having been torn into fragments and distributed among all conscious beings.

In the myth of Osiris (Egypt), the godman is murdered and dismembered by his evil brother Set. The goddess Isis collects the separated parts and reconstructs the godman from which she conceives Horus, the "Son of God". This myth encodes the Mystery teaching that God needs to be "re-membered". Out of which the Christ is born – in consciousness.

The spiritual path is the process of the reuniting the fragments of the universal daemon, of perceiving one in all. Gnostic Christians believed each individual human self to be a fragment of one single heavenly being, which had been dismembered by evil forces, robbed of all memory of its heavenly origins and forced into individual bodies. Gnostic initiates understood that identification with the body was spiritual death. To be reborn into eternal life required remembering who one was and by mystical resurrection would become the Christ who is the eternal witness that is forever unborn and undying.

INITIATION

Pagan and Gnostic philosophical systems described four levels of human identity:

1. Physical – The body

2. Psychological – The counterfeit spirit

3. Spiritual - Spirit

4. Mystical – Light power

The eidolon is number 1 and 2.

The daemon is number 3 and 4.

The Gnostics called those who identified with their body as "hylics", the term for unconscious matter (hyle).

Those who identified with their personality or "psyche" were known as "psychics".

Those who identified with Spirit were called "pneumatics", which means "spirituals".

Those who ceased to identify with lower levels of consciousness experienced Gnosis. This mystical enlightenment transformed the initiate into a true Gnostic or Knower.

In Paganism and Christianity these levels of awareness were symbolized with the four elements: earth, water, air, fire. This understanding was encoded in the cross.

Initiations leading from one level to another were called "elemental baptisms".

1. Baptism by water – transformation of the hylic from body identification to psychic identity (personality – psychic).

2. Baptism by air – transformation from psychic to pneumatic.

3. Baptism by fire – transformation to the light power – the Christ within. The baptism leading to Gnosis.

These three levels of understanding can be characterized as: Literal, Mythical and Mystical.

Literal – The Outer Mystery baptism understood that Jesus was a historical figure who literally returned from the dead. This is a pseudo history for spiritual beginners.

Mythical – The Inner Mystery of air brought the understanding that Jesus was an allegorical myth. This is the spiritual path to be traveled by each initiate.

Mystical – The final initiation whereby the initiate transcended the need for any teaching, thus becoming the Christ.

The Jewish Mysteries

The process of integration between Jewish and Pagan culture had been going on for centuries. The history of the Jews is one of repeated conquest by other nations:

1. 922 BCE – The Egyptians
2. 700 BCE – The Assyrians
3. 586 BCE – The Babylonians
4. 332 BCE – Alexander the Great
5. 198 BCE – The Syrians
6. 63 BCE – The Romans

The Jewish people in every conquest were taken into slavery and hauled off to foreign lands. This is called the "Diaspora". In the years that followed each conquest many Jews, having earned their freedom, were allowed to return to Judea. The majority chose not to return to their native home. Why? What they learned was much more dynamic than their tribal religion.

In Babylon they learned astrology. They practiced the Mysteries of Tammuz, the Babylonia version of Osiris-Dionysus. In Syria they practiced the Mysteries of Adonis, a god-man nearly identical to Jesus. They were even expelled from Rome for attempting to introduce the Pagan Mysteries of Sabazius.

Only the lower class, the Jews left in Judea, clung to the ancient tribal God Jehovah. Most Jews embraced paganism in their exile. The view that Jews were united in their opposition to paganism is a lie fostered by the literalists.

The greatest integration of Jews into pagan cultures occurred in Alexandria in Egypt. Alexander the Great conquered Egypt at the end of the 4th century BCE. The Jews had helped Alexander working as both spies and mercenaries. Being allowed to have their own quarter in the new city of Alexandria was rewarded to them. This initiated a mass migration of Jews from around the Middle East. At one time nearly one half of the population of Alexandria was Jewish. Alexandria was to be a small Greece in Egypt. A library and museum were created as the greatest statement of learning in the ancient world, replacing even Athens.

The Jews could not help coming under the spell of the Alexandrian culture, which was sophisticated and highly educated. Not surprisingly, large numbers of Jews broke with their Jewish traditions and integrated themselves into pagan society. In short order they abandoned their native language and adopted the universal Greek language. Aramaic and Hebrew were spoken as a result of continued immigration, but Greek was the dominant language and writing. It was throughout the Mediterranean.

In 325 CE, Eusebius, the Church's first propagandist, was ordered by the Emperor Constantine to create a history and creed for the Christian people. Knowing nothing of the Christian tradition of some 325 years, Eusebius seized on a description of what he thought was Christianity in a book written by Philo, a Jewish pagan student of Pythagoras (a early Pagan Mystic). Philo had referred to a certain group of Jews in Alexandria as the "Therapeutae". Philo was writing of their spring festival reminiscent of the Christian celebration of Easter. Eusebius thought he had found the earliest Christians in Alexandria.

In the spring, all over the pagan world, the pagans celebrated the dying and resurrecting godman. Of course Eusebius's discovery of the Therapeutae of 10 CE, was 20 years before the supposed crucifixion of

Jesus. The Therapeutae were pagan Jews not Christians. They were practicing the pagan story of the dying and resurrecting god-man, which had been practiced for centuries. What Eusebius was not literate enough to know was that the hero of the Jewish Mystery myth is a composite of many mythical characters. Jesus is the synthesis of two pre-existing mythical figures: the pagan godman and the Jewish Messiah.

The Hebrew word for Messiah means "Anointed" which in Greek is "Christ". Kings and high priests were anointed. The Inner Mystery initiates were anointed. The Jewish Messiah, an invention of the Jews while in Babylon, came to be seen as a supernatural figure whose arrival would herald the end of time. The Jewish Messiah gradually became integrated with the dying and resurrecting godman. The Jewish Messiah was expected to be a warrior king who would come to liberate Judea from her enemies and re-establish the line of David. But Jesus announces at his trial that, "My kingdom is not of this world."

Hellenized Jews in Alexandria, in the third and fourth centuries BCE, translated Jewish scriptures into Greek. This gave them the opportunity to create similarities between Jewish mythology and pagan mythology, which were not there beforehand. For example, in Isaiah, it was said " a young woman will conceive and give birth to a son", in the Greek this is stated, " a virgin will conceive and give birth to a son", bringing the concept in line with the pagan idea of the virgin birth.

The pagan mystery godmen were clearly mythological figures whose biographies existed "out of time" in the world of dreams and images. So why is the Jesus Story different?

Jews expected the Messiah to be a historical warrior king who would destroy their enemies. The Jewish godman was given the name Joshua/Jesus after the prophet of Exodus, Joshua Ben Nun, whose name means "Jesus son of the fish". The time chosen for his birth was linked to an important astrological event in 7 BCE. This was the stellar conjunction of Pisces. Thus the Jewish godman, Jesus becomes the new savior for a New Age – the Age of Pisces.

In 66 CE Jews in Judea revolted against Rome. Of some 3,000,000 Jews in Judea approximately 1,000,000 were killed and 100,000 sold into slavery. Traditional Judaism was in its final days since 63 BCE when the corrupt temple priests had invited Rome into their society to settle disputes. The Romans, in 70 CE, destroyed Jerusalem and many Jews felt completely betrayed by their tribal god Jehovah.

The crisis in Judaism threw up many would-be Messiahs, all of whom failed. These men, known as zealots or bandits, combined the role of political revolutionary and religious fanatic in a way comparable to modern Muslim fundamentalists. Many of these would-be Messiahs took the name of Joshua/Jesus. Some tried to repeat the miracle of the Exodus and were slaughtered.

The Jesus Mysteries presented to Jews a mythical alternative, a way of restoring meaning to their shattered lives, rekindling some pride in their national identity, and integrating themselves into the wider pagan society. The warrior Messiah gradually became the spiritual Messiah who could set each individual free through Gnosis. Within 100 years the pagan godman, designed to introduce the pagan godman to the Jews, was actually bringing the Jewish traditions to the pagans!

Jesus was destined not to remain a Jewish Messiah but to become a Universal Savior. Paul failed in his attempts to bring the Jesus Story to the fundamental Jews. A Messiah who was crucified as a common criminal was not the savior the Jews were looking for. When Paul turned to the Greeks, he at once achieved extraordinary success. Christ appeared to Greeks as a hero. Christianity to the Greeks was a hero cult devoted to a Jewish Messiah. A complete reversal was underway.

By the middle of the second century the Jesus Mysteries had been largely rejected by the Jewish community but embraced by the Gentiles. Jesus was no longer viewed as coming to save the Jews, but as coming to save the whole human race. Gentile Christians rejected the old Jewish traditions, as Paul had desired. It was at this time that Christianity began to split into camps – the Literalists and the Gnostics.

After 70 CE when Rome laid waste to Jerusalem, Jews were spread all over the Roman Empire as slaves and refugees. Most would have had, at best, the Outer Mysteries story, taking the "biography" of Jesus with them. They were cut off from Alexandria and the rest of the Empire and were prevented from completing the process of initiation. There were no masters within hundreds of miles. Within a few decades the Western Christians developed a literal belief system. They no longer viewed the Gospels as allegory, but fact. The overseers (bishops) taught that salvation was guaranteed to anyone who simply believed the story of Jesus to be literally true. This of course became the Roman Catholic Church, located in the shadows of the autocratic Roman Empire, which it emulated.

The Gnostics, who had created the Jesus Story in the first place, were now accused of perverting the sacred teachings of the savior. Irenaeus, the mouthpiece of Literalism, protested that Gnostics "overthrow the faith of many, by drawing them away under the pretense of superior knowledge." Conflict was inevitable and the battle for Christianity was on.

What had started, as a timeless myth encoding perennial teachings, now appeared to be a historical account of a once-only event in time. It was inevitable that sooner or later it would be viewed as a historical fact and a whole new religion would come into being – a religion based on history not myth, on blind allegories. It would be a religion of outer mysteries without inner mysteries. A religion based on form without content, a belief system without knowledge.

From the beginning of its history right up to the present day, Christianity has been a religion of schism and conflict. There is not a single document in the New Testament that does not warn of false teachers or attacks other Christians. At the end of the second century the Pagan satirist, Celsus writes: "Christians, it is needless to say, utterly detest each other. They slander each other constantly with the vilest forms of abuse, and cannot come to any sort of agreement in their teaching."

In the first century, the battles were over the relationship of the Jesus Mysteries to traditional Judaism. By the middle of the second century they were between the Gnostics and the Literalists. At the end of the second century various letters attributed to the apostles Peter, John and James were forged to advance Literalism and portray the Gnostics as heretics.

By the end of the second century, the Literalists had begun to establish rules for who was and who was not a Christian: a Christian must confess the Literalist creed (Nicean Creed), be baptized, and above all obey the bishops.

For the Gnostics however, the true Church was "invisible" and only its members could perceive who belonged and who didn't. Gnostics insisted that it took more than baptism to become a Christian. Reciting a creed or even martyrdom didn't make one a Christian. The Gnostics adopted the Jesus saying, "By their fruits you shall know them."

Literalist bishops saw Gnostics as a threat to their authority. Attacks on Gnosticism became fanatical and extreme calling the Gnostics, "agents of Satan". In response the Gnostics called the Literalists Church authorities, "vulgar and ecclesiastical".

In the first few centuries CE there really was no such thing as "the Church". There were competing factions, of which the Literalists were one. Justin Martyr (a Literalist), Marcion (a Gnostic) and Valentinus who tried to heal the division between the two, were all important Christian teachers in Rome at exactly the same time. Valentinus was by far the more popular.

Christian movements bearing Valentinus and Marcion's name flourished for centuries.

All Gnostic teachers commanded respect up and until their violent suppression in the fourth and fifth centuries. Valentinus was a highly

THE GNOSTICS

educated Alexandrian philosopher and poet and was elected Bishop of Egypt.

There only became a thing called "orthodoxy" when Literalist Christianity was adopted as the state religion of the Roman Empire. Even then Gnosticism continue to flourish for centuries. Orthodoxy only reflected the views of the bishops not the educated.

By the middle of the second century most Christians were Gentiles, not Jews. Most Gnostics wanted to completely reject the Jewish God Jehovah in favor of the mystical conception of God as the supreme Oneness, identical to the God of Plato and the pagan mysteries. For the sage Marcion, "Jehovah was a barbarian, and the Old Testament merely a catalog of his crimes against humanity. Christianity was a new revelation of the good God, a universal doctrine, which had nothing to do with the imperfect creed of one small nation". Even the Literalists rejected the traditions of Judaism.

Literalists wanted Jewish scripture, but not Judaism. The Literalist rearranged and changed Jewish texts to form what is today called the "Old Testament". These scriptures were arranged in such a fashion to lead directly into the New Testament and the fulfillment of the gospels.

As Literalist Christianity became more and more Roman, so the blame for the death of Jesus was shifted from the Roman governor Pilate to the Jewish nation as a whole. Bishop Melito of Sardis (170 CE) denounced the Jews as "God killers", and indeed had brought their sufferings upon themselves.

While the Jews were increasingly vilified, traditions were fabricated which portrayed Pontius Pilate as a just and holy man – even a Christian! By the fourth century both Pilate and his wife were honored as saints! This is how ludicrous and contradictory the history of early Christianity actually is.

The first attempt at constructing a Christian canon was supposedly made by Papias of Hierapolis in 110 CE. There is clearly no New Testament in Justin Martyr's time (150 CE). At the end of the second century, Irenaeus reviews canonizing the four gospels claiming they came directly from Jesus disciples, which is ironic because in Mark and Luke, neither even pretend to be eye witnesses to the events they describe!

Martyrdom

For the Literalists, Jesus had been a martyr. Therefore to meet one's death as a martyr was to follow in Jesus footsteps. Literalist martyrs were idealized as spiritual athletes and holy warriors in much the same was as Muslim extremists are today. To be martyred was to be guaranteed a place in heaven. As a result many Literalists actively sought their death saying, "By suffering for one hour one can purchase eternal life".

Gnostics viewed this martyrdom as a total misunderstanding of Christianity. Spiritual enlightenment was to be found through a mystical realization of Gnosis, not grand gestures and certainly not by suicide! Just saying "We are Christian" when one doesn't know who Christ is, is a complete misunderstanding. A human death does not lead to salvation. Those who advocate human sacrifice are making God into a cannibal.

The Gnostics did not believe that Jesus literally died as a martyr, but that his symbolic death represented a profound mystical truth: to die to one's lower self and resurrect to the Christ within.

The traditional history of persecution of Christianity paints the Roman Empire as having a particular hatred for Christianity. This is not true. Rome was constantly entertaining and purging itself of mystics, philosophers and religious cults, if seen as a threat to stability.

As early as 186 BCE the Mysteries of Dionysus had been prohibited in Rome and the shrines destroyed throughout Italy. Huge numbers of initiates were executed, many thousands at a time. Literalist Christians adopted some of these happenings as if they were their own.

THE GNOSTICS

Until the middle of the third century there were no legal persecutions of the Christians. Previously, certain individuals had been persecuted in particular cities for crimes against other religions. In the second century the Emperor Trajan warned the provinces to give all Christians a fair trial. Christians had been vandalizing other temples and shrines. They were repeatedly warned before action was started. Never the less the early records do not conform death sentences and Christianity was not perceived as a threat to Rome.

In 250 CE a plague swept the ancient world, decimating whole populations. The Empire was on the verge of collapse, and the Christian cult found itself being a scapegoat for Roman misfortunes. There were three persecutions under three Emperors covering a total of five years. The Literalists wildly exaggerated most of these persecutions. Origen, a reliable historian, tells us that "few" Christians died for their faith and were "easily numbered". In the persecutions of Alexandria, only 10 men and 7 women suffered for being Christians".

Ironically, it was Christians themselves who often courted martyrdom. One such group in Asia Minor begged the governor to put them to death, but he refused. Some Roman Emperors were actually sympathetic toward the Christians. Once Constantine declared Christianity as the state religion of Rome all persecutions and martyrdom immediately stopped.

Once Constantine endorsed Christianity as the state's only religion, Gnosticism's days were numbered. The Literalist Church began to brutalize pagan priests into recanting their gods. Priests were chained to their shrines and left to starve to death. By 386 CE, bands of mad monks, frenzied with fundamentalism, were running amok throughout the Empire, completely beyond the control of the law. On June 16, 391, the Emperor Theodosius issued an edict that closed down all pagan temples. The incredible temple of Seraphis in Alexandria was destroyed to its foundation.

An imperial decree went forth: "Burn all books hostile to Christianity lest they cause God anger and scandalize the pious." To this end illiterate monks destroyed thousands of years of accumulated wisdom and scientific knowledge as so much Pagan superstition.

In 415 CE, Archbishop Cyril of Alexandria had his monks incite a Christian mob to murder the last pagan scientist of the Alexandrian Library, a brilliant high priestess female named Hypatia. She was literally torn limb from limb and the Catholic Church sainted Cyril.

The once proud city of Alexandria, the center of the greatest empire of the ancient world, had flourished for a thousand years under its own gods. Within a few decades of turning to Christianity, the bishops and monks had destroyed all the wonders and achievements of antiquity. Christianity did not succeed as the "one" religion of the Roman Empire; in fact it accompanied the Empire's downfall. In fact Christianity prevented the rise of consciousness for 1,000 years! (The Dark Ages). What began as a message of freedom and equality ended up creating an authoritarian and despotic regime of its own.

The wanton destruction of our pagan heritage is the greatest tragedy in the history of the Western world. The Roman Church imposed its creed with threats and violence, denying generations of human beings the right to think their own thoughts and find their route to spiritual salvation. The next 1,000 years would see the death of some 200,000,000 in the name of Christianity!

Only a century ago most "thinking people" believed that the story of Adam and Eve was literally true. Darwin's idea of natural evolution was regarded as ridiculous and heretical. And all such books were banned from schools. Today it seems outrageous to claim that Christianity evolved from paganism and the Jesus story, like Genesis, is an allegorical myth.

Scholarly work, without prejudice, tells another story. Christianity did not arrive as a unique divine intervention. It evolved from the past, like everything else. The ancient pagan mysteries did not die. They are encoded within the pages of Christianity itself. Once exposed to the light of truth Literalist Christianity must die thus bringing us back to where we left of some 1,000 years ago.

THE GNOSTICS

Christianity is only one chapter in the perennial human quest for meaning. God did not come to Earth on a once-only excursion. Nor do we have to wait for his promised apocalyptic return. The truth is...God never left!

The Basic Difference Between Gnosticism and Literalism:

<u>Gnosticism</u>	<u>Literalism</u>
Mystic Individualists	Rigid Authoritarian
Different Beliefs	Common Creed
Hundreds of Gospels	Four Gospels
Mystical Knowledge	Bishop Determined Dogma
Allowed All Beliefs	Suppressed Beliefs
Oneness	Separation

Chapter Five

DECEPTIONS AND MYTHS OF THE BIBLE

Ten years ago I came across a book entitled <u>Deceptions and Myths of the Bible</u> by Lloyd M. Graham. The following are a few highlights from this important contribution.

There are just two (2) principles in the Universe:

1. Consciousness

2. Energy

These two principles are bound together throughout the entire creative process. Without energy, consciousness can do nothing. Energy without consciousness will do nothing constructive. This alone explains earthquakes, volcano eruptions, hurricanes, tornadoes, floods, forest fires, etc. These are not conscious "acts of God" but only planetary functionalism. These "acts" are no more and no less than energy acting without consciousness.

From this we can see that the "mystery of life" is man-made not God made. When an ignorant "priesthood" introduced the supernatural into a perfectly natural universe, it threw confusion into mankind. The result has been a myriad of warring religions and philosophies.

Creation implies action, and energy is the active agent. Pre-creation implies energy not in action, that is, motionless. This is the nature of non-manifesting space, the ultimate source. In metaphysics it is called THE ABSOLUTE. In scripture it is called "the deep", "without form and void".

Space is the field of cosmic manifestation- suns, planets, and moons (congealed energy). The time and means of this congregation and condensation constitute the creative process of the worlds, a matter not of solar days but of cosmic days. God did not create the world in 7 solar days but 7 cosmic days, meaning a long, long time. Primordial energy (energy existing at the beginning) cannot become dense matter in "time" as we understand it. In passing through intermediate stages, energy becomes more and more substantial eventually becoming chemical. This being the process we might say that the earth is a precipitate of primordial substance and a coagulation of cosmic energy. The cosmic clock taking millions of years to create.

Energy itself is neither constructive nor purposive. It must have a guiding, directing intelligence. That intelligence on earth is called- GENETIC. One might say the Gene-sis of our origin.

It is one vast No-thing materially, all things potentially. This is the true beginning and therefore the beginning of Truth. And so it was for all ancient races except one – the Hebrews. The Hebrew priesthood personified, deified and endowed this silent waste with wisdom, moral perfection and even self-consciousness. The greatest mistake mankind has ever made, for it confused human thought, was to divide the race into thousand of sects thus sowing the seeds of unending warfare.

The glory of creation lies in its consummation not in its inception. Consummation is perfected humanity. In "time" man becomes divine, and so man makes divinity not divinity makes man. (Voltaire, the French philosopher and scientist, was once quoted as saying; "In the beginning God created man in His image...and man promptly re-turned the favor!").

The authors of scripture did not understand that "divinity" is not a cause but the effect of evolutionary forces therefore they put divinity at the wrong end of Being. For divinity to become factual on earth, it must first become functional in man. This is the goal of evolution, and the purpose of man, both of which were concealed from us by priestly falsehoods.

In all ancient cosmologies there were seven stages in the creative process, each producing a different element and rate of vibration. The three highest elements were beyond our comprehension; they were called "spirit" in lieu of knowledge. The three planes below these were called: The Mental- The Astral – The Etheric. These three planes or elements were called The Planetary Elements to distinguish them from the Chemical Elements. In the coagulation process these six elements became number seven– DENSE MATTER.

When hydrogen becomes helium, it is no longer hydrogen. When helium becomes lithium it is no longer helium. So it is with planetary elements. When the Involutionary process becomes Dense Matter, there no longer exists what came before.

Qualities – According to scripture all "good" qualities come from God and all "evil" qualities come from Satan. The priesthood little knew that these two are one. The wiser pagans knew it and reduced it to: *Demon est Deus inversus*, meaning: the devil is God inverted. In other words, when spirit becomes matter, it becomes evil, or the source of evil. It only means that once spirit becomes dense it is no longer spirit. It must now go through an evolutionary process to return to its source. Evil spelled backwards is live. This is the return to the Garden of Eden. This is the Tree of Life.

The pagans also knew that human desire, the cause of our evil, was in the planetary elements (*desidero*) meaning from "star matter". This human desire and the stars are the same substance: Astral Matter. This the scriptures admonish us to overcome, to Master (aster-star stuff- with a prefix M). "Overcoming" in scripture is salvation through the priesthood, it is Evolution in metaphysics.

Here we see the results of false theologies. By attributing all morality and virtue to the creator of soulless, senseless matter, the priesthood hid from us the true nature of causation and the purpose of our being.

Just as all qualities man will ever need are developed in evolution, past present and future, so are the powers he will need. Through eons of conflict with a savage environment, the astral element was qualified to become our psyche, the source of psychic powers. We can arouse this power through emotion and prayer. As man's four elements are affinitized with the planets four elements, effects are sometimes possible which to the ignorant seem like omniscient responses.

This the authors of scripture did not know and so every psychic phenomenon, dreams and visions were a communication from God, Jehova. Carl Jung would call this tapping into the aura of the planet or the collective conscious of the planet. The Hindus call this the Akashic record.

Laws – There are no laws of God or laws of nature. An atom unites with another atom not because of some law but because of energy content. The interacting of elements gives rise to "relationships". These interactions give rise to constancy and man's perception of constancy, which he puts into words and calls it a "law". Thus man is the lawmaker, not God.

God makes possibilities, potentialities, while man interprets their function and makes laws to govern them. Laws are neither causative nor creative, nor do they pre-exist things. They come into being with being and being is the result of IDEATION, not laws.

As to the great mystery – time and space – The creative principle does not make time and space and put worlds into them, it "makes" worlds and time and space in the absolute. These are abstract ideas made "real" or relative only in the mind of the perceiver. The world is in the perceiver not the other way around.

The "divine lawgiver" is but man's substitute for knowledge of celestial dynamics. What man attributes to God is but the equilibration of cosmic forces. Proliferation is but the result of genetic fruitfulness.

Biologic Forms – Plant, Animal, Man - (The Kingdoms). Where did they come from? Did they come out of "congealed energy"? Out of "dead matter"? Did they arrange themselves into mutually independent sequences?

The kingdoms were part of Planetary Ideation. When the energy came forth the ideas came forth as well? The very word evolution means a coming out. The "idea" comes out of energy. In Involution (the coming forth of the elements) the "form ideas" were awakened in those elements as archetypes. Man for example is not an evolved animal nor a special creation, but only a special ideation (archetype) among many. This is key to the Kingdom forms. For over 2,000 years we have misunderstood Genesis. Even today we make fools of ourselves over it with arguments between religionists and scientists, both of which should know better.

Cosmic Forces – In spite of our enlightenment, millions today still believe that God controls the weather, when actually it is the sun. Even climate is due solely to the relationship of the sun and earth. In like manner millions today believe God created the world, when again it was the sun, but not our present sun, and nor as our science presents it. A sun is a transmitter of cosmic energy into chemical matter – congealed energy.

Prior to this, creative energy is an invisible energy and quite unknown or recognizable. From creative energy we get sun, planets, moons, asteroids etc. These are not separate but only different stages in one purposive process – the making of a life-bearing planet. This is the goal of all cosmic bodies.

At the seventh level of creation the sun constitutes the higher subdivision of this seventh plane and its work is that of transforming the primal gas into the many mineral compounds. In this way the sun is laying down within itself the physical basis of a future planet. This process is called fusion, and by means of it, the elements in the atomic table are created.

A sun is a cosmic crucible in which the cross, called matter, is made. In other words, a transmitter of cosmic energy, the sun, was a fact known thousands of years ago and reduced to many myths. The sun is laying down within itself a future moon, a slag pile left by the solar furnace in the creation of the mineral kingdom.

When the old sun dies it becomes a planet, but not for millions of years. It wanders in space, cooling, becoming a cosmic bomb, radioactive and deadly. In time it is picked up magnetically, not gravitationally, by the forces of another sun and thus a solar system is formed. It was a sun that created the world and not the God of Genesis.

All this the Ancients knew and left to the world in what we call Ancient Wisdom. The priestly founders of both Judaism and Christianity knew this, and out of it they fashioned their scriptures and religions. That accomplished they destroyed every trace of their source material or it went up in smoke with the Library of Alexandria.

That is why it is unknown to us today.

PART TWO

THE PREPARATION

CHAPTER SIX

CONSCIOUSNESS

Consciousness is normally called "states of consciousness" and takes place in four levels of brain-wave activity: Beta, alpha, theta and delta. These levels all have a measurable frequency range.

The beta level consciousness (14 to 27 cycles per second) is the waking state of consciousness. Its chief function is to monitor 75% of all physical functions.

The alpha level (8 to 13 cycles per second) is the level of subconscious mind activity. This is the meditative or light hypnosis state usually experienced just prior to and after sleep.

The next level of brain activity is called the theta state (4 to 8 cycles per second) and is called the sleep state. It is the state of unconsciousness where one is unaware of what is going on around oneself. Meditative levels can reach the theta level.

The deepest level of sleep or unconsciousness is the delta level (0 to 4 cycles per second). This is the level of deep meditation, sometimes going on for days to weeks by the accomplished yogi. It is the ultimate out of body experience. The ego is completely suspended.

The study of consciousness is difficult because of its subjective and internal nature. Charles T. Tart coined the term Altered States of Consciousness (ACS) in the 1960's. ACS can occur spontaneously, or can be induced through yoga, Zen and other forms of meditation and prayer. Brain waves can also be changed from drinking alcohol, dancing, chanting, sensory deprivation, sleep deprivation, malnutrition, fasting, diet, physical and psychological traumas, birthing, staring, sex and psychotic episodes.

Orthodox science largely rejects the experiences and knowledge gained from ACS exercises many of which are spiritual and highly subjective in nature and not subject to laboratory control.

Consciousness is a vibration and therefore an energy state. As a psycho-spiritual energy, the consciousness is said to reside within the body, mind connection. It is aroused through spiritual disciplines to achieve self-realization and illumination. In Sanskrit the term for this energy is called the *Kundalini* or serpent power. The yogis tell us it is a coiled like energy, similar to a snake at the base of the spine in the root charka.

The power of the *Kundalini* is enormous and those who have experienced it say it is beyond description. The phenomenon associated with it varies. I have experienced this energy on occasion and can testify to its amazing power. My experiences included bizarre physical sensation, visions, brilliant light super lucidity, ecstasy, bliss and a sense of being the presence of the transcendent. And this I now understand was a mild experience.

Kundalini was considered a rarity in the West prior to the 1970's. The introduction of Eastern spiritual practices to the West brought the idea and the experience of this concept. A closer study of the phenomenon shows that the energy has been recognized in one form or another in Chinese, Tibetan, Egyptian and Native American cultures for thousands of years.

This consciousness expanding experience comes in different ways. First of all it can only be experienced through consciousness expansion. Any chemical or physical alteration of the mind or body is useless. Desire for a greater spiritual awareness coupled with dedicated spiritual practices are critical to the experience.

After years of meditation and yogi practice, the student may begin to feel a heat sensation at the base of the spine. This can range from intensely hot to pleasantly warm. Once awakened the energy moves up the psychic pathways of the spinal column. As it raises it activates each of the seven charkas (energy centers) on its way to the brain (crown charka). The objective is to achieve this state of conscious expansion and maintain it. This is not for entertainment. Once achieved there is no going back to the world as it appeared before the experience.

One must be prepared for the *kundalini* experience. The neural pathways of the human body are not designed to handle extreme energy boosts but can be developed with practice. Explosive awakening has resulted in psychophysical experiences ranging from physical disregard, blindness and deafness to heart attack, insanity and even death. Preparation for transformation comes with intense practice and an overwhelming desire to know God. The human state is no longer important or even necessary.

Power vs. Force
By Dr. David Hawkins

At age 38, David Hawkins (a psychiatrist and avowed agnostic) was dying from a progressive illness. As he lay dying he reflected that he didn't care about his body but his spirit was in a "state of extreme anguish and despair". "As my final moment approached the thought flashed through my mind, What if there is a God? So I called out, If there is a God, Help me NOW!

Surrendered to whatever God there might be, I went unconscious. When I awoke, a transformation of such enormity had taken place that I was dumbstruck with awe."

"The person I had been no longer existed. There was no personal self or ego left – just an Infinite Presence of such unlimited Power. It had replaced what had been "me". The world was illuminated by the clarity of an Infinite Oneness, which expressed itself in all things revealed in their immeasurable beauty and perfection."

"For 9 months, this stillness persisted. I had no Will of my own."

He was in no way able to work at his profession. He continued to report that he could function somehow in his body but didn't "think" about it. His body was healed of its affliction but his nervous system was extremely over taxed like he was experiencing too much energy. Fame, success and money were meaningless.

He began to perceive the reality that underlay personality. That the origin of emotional sickness lay in people's belief that they were their personalities. His practice gradually resumed and became huge. He treated 1,000 new patients a year. He eventually employed 50 therapists treating some 2,000 outpatients a year. He has written books, appeared on Radio and TV.

"I became only a "witness" to myself, to the greater "I", deeper than myself or its former thoughts. This led me to investigating spiritual teachings world known sages. Everything and everyone in the world was luminous and exquisitely beautiful. It became apparent that all of mankind is motivated by inner love, but has become unaware or as sleepwalkers. They were so beautiful – I was in love with everyone."

"Years were spent in inner silence, and the strength of the Presence grew. I had no personal life – my personal will no longer existed. I was an instrument of Infinite Presence; there was no such individual as "David" any longer. When I looked into the eyes of my patients I saw myself shining in their eyes. How did I get into all these bodies? I wondered."

"I became aware that in the motionless silence there are no "events" or "things" and that nothing actually "happens" because past, present and future are merely artifacts of perception. As my limited, false self dissolved into the universal Self of its true origin, there was an ineffable sense of returning home, a state of absolute peace and relief from all suffering. For it's only the illusion of individuality that is the origin of all suffering. The realization that one is the universe dissolves all suffering."

The Budda said, "Suffering is due to ignorance (unawareness). With awareness comes the awakening and with the awakening the enlightenment and with enlightenment – Infinite Peace.

"I saw that all pain and suffering arises solely from the ego and not from God. Communicated in silence to my patients they responded with miraculous healing. Catatonics suddenly began to talk. My practice became overwhelming. This is when I first encountered kinesiology."

"I was instantly amazed by the potential I saw, it was a "wormhole" between two universes – the physical and the mind and the spirit – an interface between dimensions. In a world full of sleepers lost from their source, here was a tool to recover that lost connection with the higher reality and demonstrate it for all to see."

"It was time to leave New York and the affluence that had been created. I left the world and everything in it and took up a reclusive life in a small town for 7 years. Seven years of meditation and study. It took that long to understand how I could make my ideas concrete, how to perfect a state of consciousness as an instrument."

"I lost track of what was happening in the world. In order to do research and writing, it was necessary to stop all spiritual practice and focus on the world of form. And, so, after a long, circular journey of the spirit, I returned to the most important work, which is to bring the Presence that has moved my life perhaps a little closer to the grasp of as many of my fellow human beings as I can reach."

"As the Presence begins to prevail in your life, there is no further identification with the physical body or the mind. When the mind grows silent, the thought "I am" also disappears and Pure Awareness shines forth to illuminate what one is, was and always will be, beyond all worlds and all universes – infinite and beyond time."

How does one reach this state or awareness?

1. The desire to reach this state must be intense.

2. The discipline to act with constant and universal forgiveness. Compassion toward everything especially ones own self and thoughts.

3. A willingness to hold desires in abeyance and surrender the personal will at every moment.

4. Turn over the energy behind your thoughts to your Presence. Turning over the desire to even own these thoughts no longer allows them to reach elaboration.

"Suddenly and without warning a shift in awareness will occur and the Presence will be there. The breakthrough will be spectacular, more intense than anything you have ever known – it has no counterpart in ordinary experience. It comes with the support of Love without which you couldn't survive. A moment of terror will follow as the ego clings to its existence, fearing it will become nothing. Instead, as it dies, it is replaced by the "Self", the Everything-ness, the All in which everything is known. One is total and complete beyond all identities, gender, or even humanness itself. One will never again feel suffering and death."

"What happens to the body beyond this point is immaterial. The body appears to be an "it", rather than a "me", another object like furniture in the room. It will seem comical that people will still address the body as though it was an individual person, and there is no way to explain this state of awareness to the unaware."

"The ecstasy that accompanies this condition isn't absolutely stable and there will be moments of great agony. The agony occurs because the ecstasy isn't constant. This level of awareness will ultimately be transcended, as the necessity to transcend duality is inevitable. A new level of fear may appear in which one feels God has abandoned him/her. This "dark night of the soul" is a personally directed test but you are not on your own, the Holy Spirit is there with you. This is however a giving up of illusion, a moving beyond allness or nothingness, beyond existence or non existence."

"The culmination of the inner work is the most difficult phase, where one is starkly aware that the illusion of existence that one transcends here is irrecoverable. There is no returning from this step. But, in fact, in this final apocalypse of the self, the dissolution of duality – that of existence and non-existence – dissolves in universal divinity, and no individual consciousness is left to choose. The last step is taken by God."

"Follow this fascinating journey and you'll see how easy it can be to raise your consciousness to the levels of POWER, rather than FORCE, so that you can become one of those who is awake in this world." Your life will certainly never be the same.

The kinesiological testing procedure used by Dr. Hawkins was conducted on thousands of test subjects, both individually and in groups from all parts of the world. The results were universally the same. His book, Power vs. Force is a result of those findings.

The field of consciousness referenced on the "Map of Consciousness" is non linear and beyond the Newtonian paradigm of reality. The scale provides a link between the known and the unknown, between the manifest and the unmanifest, between duality and non-duality. This comes as a shock to those who think they are totally separate from every other thing in the universe.

Newtonian Paradigm

500–1500CE. (The Dark Ages) represents the Age of Unenlightenment or the age of Catholic dominated worldview. The collapse of this 1,000-year paradigm was brought about by:

1. Expanding world trade which brought with it new ideas that challenged Medieval thinking.

2. The argument against excessive cruelty sponsored by the church.

3. Invention of the printing press.

4. A new kind of thinker – Copernicus, Galileo and Kepler – who challenged the church's position that the earth was the center of the solar system. If it wasn't then what else had the church lied about and put men to death about?

5. As the Renaissance (rebirth of consciousness) emerged, God was pushed to the periphery of everyday consciousness.

By the 16th Century man was stuck between worldviews.

By the 17th Century the West (West of Suez) was proceeding toward science and technology. The perception of God was dramatically changing. The Enlightenment or Age of Reason forever changed the way the new paradigm would look at God.

The scientific mind looked to objectify reality and ignored the symbolic or metaphysical nature of faith. Science's claim was that a thing was either factual or it was a delusion!

Enter Sir Isac Newton, the father of Physics in the 17th Century.

His starting point was mechanical not mathematical. He wished to explain the physical universe with God as an essential part of it. God, for Newton is a continuation of the natural, physical order. This governing force was gravity. It was this force that kept things in their proper place, thus preventing chaos. Like Descarte before him, Newton had no time for mystery which both equated with superstition and ignorance.

Newton wanted to purge Christianity of the miraculous. Jesus, for Newton was not God, but a man in touch with a higher ideal. Nature is the only temple of God.

The Newtonian paradigm has everything to do with "causality". For Newton and science for four centuries, causality moves in a "linear" fashion: A – B – C. This is called "deterministic linear sequence" meaning A causes B causes C. For 400 years this belief has governed the scientific method and all proofs for mathematics.

However, since Einstein and his theory of relativity, this paradigm of causality is beginning to shift. There seems to be an invisible world, according to Einstein, which is unobservable and which "informs" the world we see. This unseen world, called by Dr. Hawkins as the "attractor" field, results in the sequencing of cause from A to B to C thus creating an observable phenomenon that can be measured. All of life's experiences are subjective in origin but require objective explanation or to make sense of. Nothing is objective, only what we "make" it.

In other words, unless the mind can "make sense" (drawing the attractor field into the realm of the 5 senses) there can be no beginning or sequencing. This attractor field Dr. Hawkins diagrams as ABC, that which is informing A – B – C. The bridge between the two is CONSCIOUSNESS. It is the bridge between the possible and the impossible, the known and the unknown.

Enlightened sages for centuries have been trying to tell us (to make sense of) that beyond consciousness lies pure awareness. This is non lineal and non measurable. This is moving from A – B – C to ABC not the opposite. Spiritual evolution occurs as a result of removing obstacles and not actually acquiring anything new. Devotion enables "surrender" of the mind's vanities and cherished illusions so it progressively becomes more free and open to the light of truth.

Nonlinear learning takes place more as a result of familiarity than by logical sequenced, processed intellection. Consciousness tends to advance as an automatic consequence of having acquired new information. Each exposure to new information advances integration and therefore new insights.

Imagine if there was nothing "private", that everything could be measured to determine its credibility? Imagine that anyone, anywhere could tell the truth about anyone, anything or everything in time and space? (If accomplished, there would be no human ego).

The book, Power vs. Force was tested. Every sentence was tested. The book calibrated in the 800's. Without any formal marketing, only word of mouth, the book has gone world wide and in many translations and is used by study groups in colleges, universities and research departments.

Interest in the book has come from primarily spiritually interested groups as well as from healers. So far the interest is not mainstream mainly because mainstream consciousness is not that far along (85% of the world's consciousness is below 200).

The very people this procedure would help the most are not prepared to use it.

Kinesiology – The study of the forces that produce motion. From the Greek – meaning movement. *Kinesiology* (applied *kinesiology*) first received scientific attention in the 1850's through the work of Dr. George Goodheart. His work focused on how various substances would cause indicator muscles to go strong or weak. Somehow, at a level far below conceptual consciousness, the body "knew" what was good or bad for it.

In the late 1970's, Dr. John Diamond began testing emotional and intellectual stimuli (behavioral *kinesiology*) as well as physical stimuli. A "smile" for example will test "strong" while a "I hate you" will test "weak".

Testing Method (It takes two persons above the 200 consciousness level to work the system)

1. Have the "subject" stand erect, right arm relaxed at his side. Left arm held out parallel to the floor, elbow straight.

2. Face the subject; place your left hand on the subject's right shoulder. Place your right hand on the subject's extended left arm, just above the wrist.

3. Tell the subject to resist as you push his arm down. Not ridged.

CONSCIOUSNESS

4. Push down on subject's arm fairly quickly, firmly and evenly. You are testing the spring and bounce in the arm. Not hard but hard enough to lock the shoulder joint.

5. Have subject close their eyes.

6. No music playing in the background.

7. Remove eyeglasses.

8. Testing arm free of jewelry.

9. Speak in your normal voice and don't prejudice your feelings.

Demonstration

1. Ask the subject to hold an image in mind while being asked to "resist". Let's say the mental image is a person. Let's say the person is Jesus Christ. How does the subject test?

2. Now ask the subject to hold in mind the personality of Adolf Hitler. Ask the subject to "resist". What happened

3. Have the subject hold in mind a time they were angry, jealous, depressed, guilty or fearful. Test the subject. What happened? Now have the subject hold in mind a loving person, situation or object of affection. Test. Results?

4. Now hold a picture of a substance in mind. Let's say Burbon Whiskey. Now hold an image of bottled water. Results?

The critical response point is 200.

Above this point is considered "strong", while below this point is considered "weak".

1. Refer to the scale when calibrating. Say, "On a scale of 1 to 1,000, where 200 is the level of integrity or truth, this _____ calibrates at _____."

2. Have subject hold a book in their right hand. Ask, "is this book over 100"? Over 300? Over 400? You can calibrate anything using this procedure. Two sensitive partners can calibrate anything to the exact level of truth. Tester and subject may trade places and should get the same results.

3. Once two people become familiar with the technique, test any subject: movies, individuals, historical events, and politicians.

Type of Questions

1. Make declarative statements about existing conditions or events. Questions that require a "yes" or "no" answer

2. Don't ask questions about the future.

3. Be impersonal. Don't prejudice the response.

4. Do not use the words "good" or "bad" as they are relative and confusing to the subject.

5. Do not ask personally compromising questions.

6. All motivation must have integrity.

7. The thymus thump can stabilize testing. A couple of thumps while smiling and thinking of something positive. Saying out loud "Ha-Ha-Ha".

MAP OF CONSCIOUSNESS

All levels below 200 are destructive to life in both the individual and society at large and are a force of consciousness not a power of consciousness. Levels above 200 are constructive expressions of Power. Therefore the level 200 is the fulcrum that divides the general areas of force and power.

Anyone's consciousness is a truth average, because personality tends to act differently in different situations. One might be at 150 in his marriage and 250 with his friends. This would result in an average 200 consciousness or energy level.

Energy Levels

20 – Shame – A feeling of being a non-person. This is a feeling of being close to death or severe abandonment. Early childhood trauma (abuse) produce great neurosis resulting in low self esteem. Usually shy, withdrawn and introverted. Consciousness in the 20's is dangerous. This level on consciousness is prone to hallucination and paranoia. Psychotic behavior often ensues.

Some Shame-based individuals become perfectionists, intolerant and driven. Moral extremists are examples of Shame based individuals. They project their own unconscious shame on others so they can attack them. Serial killers act out of sexual moralism thus punishing "bad" women. Since it pulls down the whole level of personality, Shame results in a vulnerability to the other negative emotions, and, therefore often produces false pride, anger, and guilt.

30 – Guilt – Commonly used to manipulate and punish. It expresses itself as remorse, self-recrimination, masochism and all versions of victim hood. Unconscious Guilt results in psychosomatic disease, being accident prone and suicidal behavior.

It is the domain of the "sin-and-salvation" merchants who are obsessed with punishment. Those who are either acting out their own guilt or are projecting it on to others.

Guilt provokes rage and killing is frequently its expression. Advocates of Capital Punishment are those who project their guilt on others.

50 – Apathy – Characterized by poverty, despair and hopelessness. The world and the future look bleak. Pathos is the theme of life. This is the consciousness of the homeless and the derelicts of society. It is also the fate of most of the aged who become isolated with chronic diseases.

Apathy is the level of abandonment of hope.

75 – Grief – The Level of sadness, loss and dependency. Most of us have experienced this level at some time. It is the level of mourning, bereavement and remorse about the PAST. It is the level of habitual losers and gamblers – those who accept failure as a lifestyle.

Grief is the cemetery of life. But yet it's better than apathy. When one begins to cry they are getting better.

100 – Fear – Fear runs much of the world. It is the basic motivator for most people. It limits the growth of the personality and leads to inhibition. It takes energy to rise from fear and the truly oppressed are unable to do so without help.

125 – Desire – Motivator for most of human activity and most economies. Goal motivator. It is the level of addiction, the level where craving becomes more important than life itself.

Desire is the basis of accumulation and greed. There is never enough at this level. It is easy to get stuck here. If properly understood Desire can springboard us to yet higher levels of awareness.

150 – Anger – Anger can lead to either constructive or destructive action. Anger expresses itself most often as resentment and revenge. It is a volatile and dangerous energy, exemplified by irritable, explosive people who become "injustice" collectors. Wants arising from desires not being filled creates frustration. Anger leads easily to hatred, which erodes all areas of a person's life.

175 – Pride – The first level of feeling positive about oneself. This level gives rise to self-esteem and a sense of being worth more rather than worth less. Pride is defensive and vulnerable because it is dependent upon external conditions, without which it can suddenly revert to a lower level. The inflated ego is vulnerable to attack. Pride remains "weak" because it can be knocked off its pedestal back to shame, which is the threat that fires the fear of loss and pride.

Man has habitually died for Pride – armies gladly give up human life for nationalism.

The downside of Pride is arrogance and denial, which block growth. Pride must be resolved if real Power is to be attained.

<u>200 – Courage –</u> Power first appears. This is the critical line between Power and Force or the positive and negative influences of life. Sometimes called the level of integrity, honesty and truth. It is the first level of empowerment. Life becomes exciting, challenging, and stimulating.

Courage implies the "willingness" to try new things and deal with the changes and challenges of life. Up until now one couldn't deal with the opportunity of life. Now he can. Growth and education become attainable. One can look past fear and character defects and elect to go on in spite of them.

People at this level put back into the world as much as they take. This is where people and societies truly begin being productive.

The collective energy level of consciousness of mankind remained at 190 for many centuries. In 1986 a shift occurred to level 207. This was the year of the harmonic convergence.

<u>250 – Neutrality –</u> Also called the level of non-positionality, which characterizes the levels below neutrality. To be neutral means to be relatively unattached to outcomes. Not getting one's way is no longer experienced as defeating, frightening, or frustrating.

Neutrality means one has surpassed conflict, competition, or guilt. This level of consciousness is basically comfortable with self and is undisturbed emotionally. It is non-judgmental and non-controlling. Neutral people likewise can't be controlled.

<u>310 – Willingness –</u> The Gateway to higher levels. One has overcome inner resistance to life and is committed to participation. This level of consciousness is helpful to others and contributes to society. Self-esteem is high.

<u>350 – Acceptance –</u> The level of major Transformation in that one understands, finally, that he is the source and creator of his own life's experience. It is the decision to live harmoniously with all the forces of

life. It is the realization that the source of happiness is within not "out there". Love is not sought but realized. Love was never out there it was always in side.

Not to be confused with passivity, which is a symptom of apathy.

One begins to see the whole picture. Right and wrong are seen as purely relative and attention is directed to problem solving. Self-discipline and mastery are predominant.

400 – Reason – This is the level of science, medicine, and increased capacity for conceptualization and comprehension. It is the level of our great thinkers, Nobel Prize winners, statesmen, and justices. Einstein, Freud, Jung.

The downside is the failure to properly interpret the symbols. Confusion between the subjective and the objective can arise thus limiting the understanding of causality. Intellectualizing can become an end in itself.

Reason does not of itself provide a guide to truth. It produces massive amounts of information but cannot resolve discrepancies in data. Reason, paradoxically, is a major block to reaching higher levels of consciousness. Transcending this level is relatively rare in our society.

500 - Love – This is not the intense emotional condition called love by most people, which is characterized as having much to do with physical attraction, possessiveness, control, addiction, eroticism, and novelty. If love can turn to hate, love never existed in the first place. Hate stems from pride not love.

The 500 levels are characterized by a sense of unconditional, unchanging and permanent being. Love is a state of being. It's a forgiving, nurturing and supportive way of relating to the world. Love is not intellectual and does not come from the mind. Love emanates from the Heart. Reason deals with particulars. Love deals with entireties. Love is not linear. Like intuition it is instantaneous and requires no sequential symbol processing.

Love takes no position and is universal, rising above separation.

Love focuses on the goodness in life in all its expressions. This is the level of true happiness.

Only 0.4 percent of the world's population ever reaches this evolution of consciousness.

<u>540 – Joy –</u> As love becomes more and more unconditional, it begins to be experienced as inner Joy. Joy comes from within. It's the level of healing and of spiritually based self-help groups.

This begins the level of the saints and advanced spiritual students and healers. The hallmark of this level is "compassion".

Individual will merges into divine will.

One's consciousness is used for the benefit of life rather than for particular individuals. The more one loves the more one can love.

<u>600 – Peace –</u> God-consciousness. It is extremely rare on this planet. 1:10 million! This level means the distinction between object and subject has disappeared. People usually remove themselves from worldly activity. Spiritual teachers.

Characterized by an infinite silence in the mind, which has stopped conceptualizing. That which is witnessing and that which is witnessed take on the same identity. The observer dissolves into the landscape and becomes equally the observed.

Great works of art, music and architecture calibrate between 600 and 700. Called inspirational and timeless.

<u>700 – Enlightenment</u> -The level of the sage. He is the ones who bring the patterns for the rest of us. There is no longer a personal self separate from others, but an identification of the Self with Consciousness and Divinity. Beyond mind. It is the peak of the evolution of consciousness in the human realm.

There is no longer identification with the physical "I". The body is a tool of consciousness. This is the level of non-duality, of Oneness. Awareness is equally present everywhere.

The ego's definition would be "some superhuman accomplishment of your mind". Actually, it is simply one's natural state of "felt" oneness with "Being". The inability (perception) to feel this connection leads to the illusion of "separation" from yourself and the world.

Buddha – Enlightenment is the end of suffering because enlightenment is waking up to the realization that there is nothing outside of you.

Being – is not a person, place or thing but an experience. Being is a "NOW" experience. It can be felt but not understood. The experience of Being puts an end to incessant "thinking" which is the disease of the mind where you believe you are your mind rather than you use the mind.

The beginning of freedom is the realization that thinking does not possess you. The more you become the observer of experience the more you begin to wake up. Judgment prevents waking up. Judgment creates resistance, which holds the illusion in place. Judgment leads to experiencing that which you resist leads away from enlightenment.

The 700+ level of consciousness is the level of the Great Ones of history. The individual no longer exists as consciousness and is totally identified with the Self. The ego is totally transcended. This is the peak of consciousness evolution in the human realm. The level 700+ avatar affects all humanity. This is the level of pure nonduality or complete oneness. There are currently less than two-dozen sages on the planet who have achieved this level.

Those beings who have surpassed the 990 level are called "Lord" as in Lord Krishna, Lord Buddha and Lord Jesus Christ, the only three teachers to have ever calibrated at 1,000.

No human has ever calibrated over 1,000.

Chapter Seven

AWARENESS

The Power of Now
By Eckhart Tolley

Enlightenment Is The End Of Separation

The Buddha suggests that enlightenment is, "the end of suffering." And what is left when there is no suffering? Felt oneness with Being, which is the state of connectedness with something immeasurable and indestructible. The inability to feel this connection gives rise to the illusion of separation from yourself and the world around you. The feeling of separation gives rise to "conflict" which in turn gives rise to fear and a fear-based world.

Enlightenment is a state of wholeness, of being "at one" and therefore at peace. At one with what you ask? At one with Being!

Enlightenment is not only the end of suffering and conflict but the end of enslavement to thinking.

Being

The eternal One Life beyond form, which is not subject to birth and death. Being is not only beyond but also deep within every form. You cannot understand it with your mind. You can only know it when the mind is still. It is only when you are still that you are present. When you are in the present you are in the NOW.

Being can be felt but never understood mentally. Being is accessed only in the silence where the mind is not and no thoughts interfere. The felt awareness of Being is enlightenment.

God

A religious term more identified with the ego than with the divine. God is usually preceded by some pronoun such as "My" or "Our" or "Your".... At any rate the word God is a closed concept, something distant, separate and outside of you.

The word God can only point you toward something. The question is: does it point to a transcendental, invisible, silent reality or an idea in the mind, a mental idol?

The term Being has an advantage over the term God in that Being is an open concept. It doesn't reduce the infinite to a finite entity to be defined in the mind. Anything defined is limited by the definition. Being is felt awareness, which cannot be imaged or defined but only felt. Therefore no one can claim exclusive possession of it as they do with God. Until words stop, no experience can begin. To experience Being one must stop defining, talking and imaging. In other words, stop the noise, which prevents the experience.

Thinking

Identification with your mind creates an identification with concepts, labels, images, words, judgments and definitions all of which block the true relationship between you and yourself, you and your fellow man, you and nature and between you and God.

Thinking creates the illusion that there is a you and a separate "other." Thinking leads to "forgetting" which means no longer feeling the oneness between you and the world. Thinking creates "belief" which takes the place of "knowing." Belief is a mind concept, which creates comfort in a mental world.

Thinking has become a disease. Disease happens when things get out of balance. Incessant thinking is out of balance. The mind is a tool. If used properly can open up infinite possibility. If used wrongly can become very destructive. Wrongly in this sense means you are not using your mind at all, it is using you by using up your energy in useless thinking. The disease you have believes you are your mind. The mind has taken you over.

Just ask yourself the question, "Can I be free of my mind whenever I want to?" What is your answer? Have you found the off button?

The beginning of freedom is the realization that YOU are NOT THE THINKER. Once you begin to understand this you can begin observing the thinker from a higher level of consciousness. You then begin to realize that the things that really "matter" – beauty, love, creativity, joy, and inner peace – all arise from beyond mind, not through the mind. This realization is called the awakening. The result is enlightenment, the end of suffering.

The voice in your head is the accumulation of your thoughts, which are mostly out of control. However, you can free yourself from what you have created. You can escape the prison you have put yourself in. Start watching what you are thinking.

"Be" there as a witnessing presence (Be Present). Do not judge, just watch. As you begin to realize that there is a voice and there is you listening to it you will realize your "I am" presence is not thought but something arising beyond mind.

As you begin to identify with the presence, the thought begins to lose it's power over you and you begin to experience peace. When thought subsides sometimes you will notice a "gap" between thoughts. A few seconds at first, then longer. Notice what you feel in the gap. In the silence between the words, between the thoughts is what? – Peace.

This is the beginning of felt-awareness; of felt oneness; of the joy of Being; of enlightenment.

To be fully present is to be "out of your mind". This is a heightened state of consciousness, unlike sleep. As you go deeper into the realm of no-mind, you realize the state of pure consciousness. Everything pales in comparison. This is not a selfish state but a selfless state.

Another way to experience the presence is instead of watching the thinker; you can create a gap in the mind stream by focusing your attention on the NOW. Just become intensely conscious of the present moment. This is deeply satisfying and is the essence of meditation.

Being Present

When you wash your hands, walking, or any activity. Pay attention to all the details. Use your senses intently. Observe the flow of your breath. Become aware of the powerful sense of presence. The more present you become, the more at ease and peaceful you feel within. The proof is in the presence.

The single most vital step on your journey toward enlightenment is this: LEARN TO DISIDENTIFY WITH YOUR MIND. With every gap in the mind stream, the light of your consciousness grows stronger.

Ninety percent of your thinking is repetitive and useless. Most everything you obsess over never comes to anything. Obsessive thinking is usually negative and harmful to the vital energy of the body. Obsessive, compulsive thinking is an addiction. An addiction occurs when you no longer feel you have a choice to stop. An addiction gives you a false sense of pleasure that invariably leads into PAIN.

An addiction creates a sense of being identified with what you can't stop doing. You somehow believe you would cease to be if you didn't have the object of your addiction. Thinking is no different than any other addiction. As you grow up you develop a mental image of who you are based on your conditioning. This is not your real self but yourself defined self or your EGO. The ego is your mind activity and is kept going through constant thinking. You are addicted to a false self not your real self.

To the ego, the present moment hardly exists. Only past and future are considered important. The ego lives in the past from where it got its definition. The future is a projection where the ego can continue to live out its past identification. Because the ego's definition of you is false you can only be happy or at peace in the future which never comes. This is the ego's game. Even the present is viewed as the past, or at best a means to get to the future. This is why the ego created a heaven to someday get to where it will be at peace. Just observe your mind and you will see that this is how it works.

YOU CANNOT FIND THE PRESENT MOMENT AS LONG AS YOU ARE YOUR MIND.

The present moment holds the key to your liberation.

Mind is a stage in the evolution of consciousness. It is not the height to which consciousness is capable but only a step. It is time for us to move on least we become trapped by what we have created. Thought is a small part of consciousness. Consciousness is everything. Thought is just a small part of it.

To become enlightened means rising above thought, not becoming a vegetable. In enlightenment you still use your thinking mind when needed, but in a much more focused way. When you use your mind, when you are looking for a solution, oscillate every few minutes between thought and stillness, between mind and no-mind. No-mind is consciousness without thought. Thought alone is barren, insane and destructive. No-mind is the powerful essence of all that is, of pure being.

The mind is essentially a survival machine. The mind is constantly analyzing not creating. Creating comes from no-mind. Problem solving comes from no-mind. The Life Force cannot be a product of mind for it is vastly too complex. The Life Force is consciousness, which has developed a mind. Creation and evolution will take us past this point as we begin to recognize the necessity to move on.

Emotion

Emotion comes from the Latin word *"emovere"* which means to disturb.

Emotions are the body's reaction to the mind. Mind is thought and it includes your emotions as well as your mental-emotional reactive patterns. Emotions arise at the place where mind and body meet. Emotions are reflections of your mind in the body. As an example, attack thoughts create a buildup of energy in the body that results in anger, which leads to fighting.

The thought that you are being threatened causes the body to contract. Biochemical changes occur from thoughts, which are the physical aspects of emotion. Emotions that are not expressed in the body can be magnets for others to attack. Emotions seem to have an energy that attracts like energy whether expressed or hidden. Anger triggers anger no matter how provoked.

If you have difficulty feeling your emotions, start by focusing attention on the inner energy field of your body. Feel the body from within. This will also put you in touch with your emotions.

If you sense a conflict between the thought and the feeling go with the feeling. Watching an emotion is the same as watching a thought. A thought is in your head while the emotion is in your body. Instead of becoming the emotion, become the watcher of the emotion. Practicing will bring up all that is unconscious for you to release in the light of consciousness. Don't analyze, just watch. The body is the doorway into Being.

An emotion represents an amplified and energized thought pattern and it may be hard to stay present enough to watch it. It wants to take you over and usually does. You can overcome the energy by being present. If you get pulled into unconscious identification with the emotion you will become identified with the emotion and it will become you. It will take you over. Emotions are reinforced by thoughts. If the pattern knocks you unconscious you will remain that way until the leakage weakens the body and you return to your previous conscious state, which is still unconsciousness but weakened by the energy.

Basically, all emotion has its origin in "loss of awareness" of who you are beyond name and form. At your deepest level the emotion of fear colors all the emotions. The payoff is PAIN. The mind's main function is to head off this pain but only succeeds in a temporary cover up. The harder the mind tries to cover it up the stronger the feeling becomes. (What you resist persists, what you look at disappears).

Pain only goes away when you cease to be identified with it. Your sense of self is closely identified with pain, which is the ego. The ego wants you to identify with your mind and thus your pain, for not to do so would mean you are identified with Being and the ego dies. The ego is most afraid of death do to identification with Being. The mind toppled from its place of power reveals Being as your true nature.

Love, Joy and Peace

These are natural states, which have no opposite as in the case of emotions. They are inseparable from Being. They happen in the gaps of no-mind when the mind is rendered "speechless", usually triggered by moments of great beauty, extreme physical exertion or great danger.

Suddenly, there is great inner stillness wherein you experience intense joy, love and peace. Everyone has these moments. They are revelations, which occur outside of time and space. They can only become permanent when you free your mind of the noise. They are not emotions as emotions have their roots in duality, their opposites. In duality you cannot have good without bad.

Love, Joy and Peace lie beyond the emotions and are on a much deeper level. They are deep states of Being or interconnectedness with Being. They have no opposite because they arise from beyond the mind.

Pleasure is of the mind because it is always derived from outside you. Joy arises from within. The very thing that gives you pleasure today will give you pain tomorrow, or it will leave you, and therefore its absence will give you pain. In any event emotions occur in the realm of mind or the dominion or the opposites. What is usually referred to as love may be pleasurable and exciting for a while, but it is an addictive clinging, a needy condition that can turn into its opposite at the flip of a switch. Most "love" relationships are love-hate relationships, which follow the dualistic principle of attraction and attack.

Real Love doesn't make you suffer. It has no opposite and is therefore not in your mind. Likewise real Joy cannot turn into pain. Most everyone gets glimpses of these states even before they wake up. They are aspects of your true nature, which is obscured by your mind. An experience of true love, joy and peace will be excused by your mind as illusion because it wasn't lasting.

Desire

Desires or cravings are the mind seeking salvation of fulfillment in external things and in the future. As long as I am my mind, I am those desires and cravings. I am needy and in the need there is no I only the need. Even the need for enlightenment is just another craving for fulfillment. You cannot achieve enlightenment you can only become enlightened. Become present. Be here as the observer of the mind.

Humans have been in the grip of pain for eons, ever since they entered into the knowledge of the opposites. This is considered the fall from grace. The opposites can only occur in the realm of time and mind. Being is lost in time. Once humans adopted time they started to judge themselves as meaningless fragments in an alien universe, unconnected to the Source and to each other. We are trying to get back into the Garden of Eden but The angles of Desire and Fear block the way. We can get back to the Garden by becoming the watcher rather than the doer. Pain is inevitable as long as we are identified with the mind, which is to say as long as we are unconscious, spiritually speaking.

There are two levels of pain; the pain you create now and the pain from the past that still lives in the mind and body.

Create no more pain in the present

The greater part of human pain in unnecessary. It is self-created as long as the unobserved mind runs your life.

Pain comes from resistance. On the level of thought, the resistance is some form of judgment. On the emotional level, it is some form of negativity. The intensity of the pain depends on the degree of resistance to the present moment and how strongly you are identified with the mind.

The mind seeks to deny the now and escape from it. The more you identify with the mind, the more you suffer. The more you honor the Now, the more you are free of pain, of suffering and the ego mind.

Time and mind are inseparable. Mind cannot function without reference to past and future so the timeless Now is threatening to its existence.

Mind and time are needed in the world to function but they have taken over our lives, which is why we have dysfunction, pain and sorrow. An increasingly heavy burden of time has been accumulating in the human mind. All humans are suffering under this burden, and they keep adding to it when they deny the present moment or use it to get to the future, which only exists in the mind, never in actuality. The collective consciousness holds a great deal of pain from the past. To heal the pain we must stop adding to time. How? Realize the present moment is all there is. Make the Now the primary focus of your life and teach others to do the same.

Before you dwelt in time and paid brief visits to the Now, now dwell in the Now and pay brief visits to the past and future only for practicality. Calendar time requires life to function. Psychological time can be a prison if not healed in the Now. Always say yes to the present moment. It's insane to create resistance to what already is. Stop it. What could be more insane than to oppose life itself, which is Now and always Now? Surrender to what is and say yes to life- and see how life starts working for you rather than against you.

The Pain Body

As long as you are unable to access the power of Now, every emotional pain that you experience leaves behind a residue of pain that lives on in you. It merges with the pain of the past and becomes lodged in your mind and body. This accumulated pain is a negative energy field that occupies your body and mind. This is your emotional pain body. It can be dormant or active depending on the person but can be activated quite easily by a comment or random thought. Try to catch it as soon as it starts to surface. If you don't it could overwhelm you and you will literally be beside yourself in pain.

The pain body is always on the lookout for that which it feeds on: anger, destructiveness, hatred, grief, emotional drama, violence, and even illness. Once the pain body has taken you over, you want more pain. You either want to inflict pain or suffer pain, or both. This of course is unconscious but just observe what happens. Its survival depends on your unconscious identification with it, but if you do not face it you will be forced to relive it again and again. The light of consciousness will cause the pain to dissolve. The light of consciousness is the presence. No pain is possible if you are fully present. The pain comes out of the past.

The pain body counts on you buying into it to keep it going. The moment you observe it take your attention into it (become aware). When you do, the identification is broken. This awareness is called the PRESENCE. Once you become the watcher of the pain body (accepting it for what it is) it can no longer hide in you. Pain cannot live in the Now.

The moment your thinking is aligned with the pain body, you are identified with it and again feeding it with your thoughts. This identification knocks you unconscious and you become the pain body. Anger is always a sign that pain is nearby. An angry person is an unconscious, pain based person. Unless the person becomes the watcher of his pain it will not stop. You can only become the watcher of your own pain. Not buying into the pain of another will infuriate the other person even more but will diffuse the energy. You must remain present or you will get sucked in.

In Summary: Focus attention on the feeling inside you. Know that it is the pain body. Accept it being there. DON'T THINK ABOUT IT. Don't judge or analyze. Stay present. Be the observer of what is happening inside you.

Being present is the most powerful tool for transformation possible. You will never understand it; you can only experience it.

The Origin of Fear

It comes in many forms: unease, worry, anxiety, nervousness, tension, dread, phobia, etc. These are all psychological conditions. They are conditions of anticipation of something in the future. Of something that "might" happen, not something that is happening now. You are in the here and now, while your mind is in the future. Fear is in the future projection of the mind not in the Now. You cannot cope with a projection – you cannot cope with the future.

As long as you are identified with your mind, the ego runs your life. The ego is afraid. Afraid of being found out. The message the body is receiving continuously from the ego, the false mind self is DANGER. I am under threat. The emotion generated from this constant message is FEAR.

Fear seems to have many causes: fear of loss, fear of failure, fear of being hurt etc. Ultimately the ego is afraid of only one thing, DEATH or annihilation and therefore the fear of death affects every aspect of your life. You cannot even be wrong for to be wrong signals death to the ego and therefore you get angry and defend your position, sometimes to the death of the body. Wars are fought over this and countless relationships have broken off because of it. All over the world people will die to be right.

If your sense of self comes from the mind it is threatened immediately. If the sense of self comes from a deeper place in you there will be no aggressiveness or defensiveness about it. Defenses do what they defend – A Course in Miracles. There is nothing to defend but an illusion. Power over others is weakness disguised as strength. True power is within, and is available NOW. Fear is the constant companion of he who is identified with his mind. Mind identification is the opposite of being identified.

Very few on this planet have gone beyond mind and therefore the vast majority live in fear.

Wholeness

As long as the ego mind is running your life you cannot ever be at ease. Peace and fulfillment are temporary. The ego identifies with external things, which are never satisfying. It needs to be fed constantly. The most common ego identifications: possessions, job, social status, recognition, education, knowledge, physical appearance, social abilities, relationships, personal and family history, belief systems, political, nationalistic, racial, religious, and other collective identifications. NONE OF THESE IS YOU. All of these you will have to give up sooner or later. At physical death you will get it that none of these are you. The secret of life is to die before you die and therefore find that there is no death. Paul said, "I die daily".

Moving into the Now

The problem of the mind cannot be solved on the level of the mind. The mind or ego or false self is a substitute for your real self. The false self's needs are endless. The ego feels vulnerable and threatened and so lives in a state of fear and want. The ego identifies with problems and thrives on them. To solve your problems would mean a loss of self, which the ego cannot tolerate and therefore keeps the problems going to preserve the self.

This is the definition of being unconsciousness. To become conscious you simply become present. Being present allows the mind to be as it is but not getting entangled in its game. The mind is not dysfunctional. Dysfunction sets in when you seek yourself in mind and mistake it for who you are. It then becomes the ego mind and takes you over.

Time and mind are inseparable. Remove time from your mind and it stops. To identify with your mind is to be trapped in time. Trapped in time means living in your memories or anticipations which is a preoccupation with the past and future. Mind will not let the present moment be, for doing so would require no-mind to be present and this the mind will not allow.

The past creates your identity and the future promises salvation or fulfillment. Both are illusions. Focusing on past or future prevents you from being in the Now which is the most precious thing there is. There never was a time when your life was not Now, nor will there ever be. The Now is the only point that can take you beyond mind. It is the portal to Being. It is a return to the Garden.

The mind cannot understand about the Now because that is foreign to its reality. Only you can understand it, not with your mind but with your Being. "Be still and know" is the only way you will ever know. Don't speak, don't think, just listen! The moment you grasp it there will be a shift in consciousness from mind to Being, from time to presence. Suddenly, everything feels alive, radiates energy, and emanates Being.

The essence of Zen consists of walking the razors edge of Now – to be so utterly and completely present that no problem, no suffering, nothing that is not who you are in your essence, can survive you. In the Now, in the absence of time, all your problems disappear. Suffering needs time; it cannot exist in the Now. Zen teaching, "What, at this moment, is lacking?" and "If not Now, when?"

Meister Eckhart (13th Century) said "Time is what keeps the light from reaching us. There is no greater obstacle to God than time."

There is a place for mind and mind knowledge – day to day living. It's when it takes you over that it becomes dangerous. Its intention is to consume you for its purpose. There is use and there is abuse. In the west we are into obsessive thinking and anything obsessive is abuse. What is needed is a shift in consciousness. This can only happen with less focus on past and future.

Step out of time as much as possible in your everyday life. Self-observation, as previously described, creates more out of time experience called being present. The moment you realize you are not present you ARE present. Whenever you are able to observe your mind, you are no longer trapped in it. The witnessing presence is beyond the mind, beyond time and beyond definition. It is timeless.

The watcher does not judge. To judge means to hold in place. Judgment is of the ego. Watch the thought, feel the emotion, observe the reaction but do not judge. None of it is personal so don't make it personal. Once you feel this presence you will find it easier to step out of time whenever time is not needed for practical purposes.

Practical time is "clock time". You have a choice to either use your mind for practical purposes or to be consumed by the mind, which is enslavement. Enlightenment is the end of slavery to the mind. The enlightened person's main focus is on the Now, but they are still peripherally aware of time. Use clock time but do not identify with it. The problem is we identify with time and therefore build up a psychological dependency on it. It becomes an addiction just like thinking. Both are ego tools to keep us off mark, off the Now. It's clock time that creates the requirement to judge and measure. Non- judgment becomes harder with clock identification. Judgment makes forgiveness (to let go) difficult and leads to a buildup of guilt and shame.

Goal setting necessarily requires clock time. If the goal is to arrive at a greater sense of happiness, you will never succeed because no amount of clock time can resolve this needy, some-a-day reality. Setting goals, without honoring the Now will never be reached. Setting goals without sacrificing the Now are achieved but not judged. Be all you can be. Don't judge it. There is no arriving only the journey. Most goals imply a since of lack or less than you. There is no lack and you are perfect as you are.

At a deep level you know who you are and will have what you feel you deserve. In remembering who you are, what you deserve is automatic. As you wake up, your acceptance of you and your circumstances reduces your anxiety. You ultimately have everything the universe has to offer in the Now.

Psychological time is converting clock time into a self-identification. The more past and future you identify with the more negativity you accumulate in your psyche. Unease, anxiety, tension, stress, worry (fears) are caused by too much future and not enough presence. Guilt, regret, resentment, grievances, sadness, bitterness and all forms or non- forgiveness are likewise caused by to much past, and not enough presence.

Time is the cause of your suffering or your problems. There can be no salvation in time. You cannot be free in the future. You can only be free Now. You can only be saved Now.

Do not confuse your life with your "life situation". The former you are. The latter you "think" you are and are identified with. You are not your life situation. You created your life situation, which of course is an illusion. Your life situation is a statement of psychological time. You are where you are because that's where your thought brought you. To change your situation, stop your thinking about it. If you changed your thinking more of the same will continue. Forget about your life situation for a while and pay attention to your life and see what happens.

Your life situation exists in Time.

Your real life is Now.

Your life situation is mind-stuff.

Your life is real.

Your life situation is an illusion.

The narrow gate that leads to life is the Now. Narrow your life down to this moment and you will find you have no problems Now. The path is narrow. Few ever enter.

When the glass is full there is no room for anything new. Make some room; make some space so the life underneath your life situation can come through. Stop and look around. Don't judge. Just be. Just for a moment. Use your senses fully. Don't think but feel. See the colors and textures. Be aware of the space everything is in. Listen to the sounds. Listen to the silence underneath the sounds. Touch something – feel and acknowledge its Being. Observe the rhythm of your breath. Allow everything to simply be and move into the Now. As you do you leave behind the dead world of mental abstraction of time. As you do you awake out of the dream of time into the present.

If you focus your attention on the Now what problems do you have at the moment? It is impossible to have a problem when your attention is fully in the Now. When you focus on the problem you are focused on the future. You become overwhelmed by you life situation and you lose your sense of life, of Being. When you create a problem, you create pain. When you stop the problems, you stop the pain. You won't make that choice unless you are truly fed up with the suffering. Have you had enough? If you create no more pain for yourself, you create no more pain for others. Without pain consciousness is advanced. The paradigm shift occurs, time ends and the world is healed. This is our only chance of survival as a race.

Ask yourself: Is there joy, ease, and lightness in what I am doing? If not, then time is covering up the present moment and life is perceived as a burden or a struggle. Focus on the doing rather than on the arriving. Accept what is thereby not resisting the Now. Allow what you are doing to be all there is in the moment. Honor the present moment and all unhappiness and struggle will dissolve. Joy and ease surface from beyond the mind.

Acting out of present-moment awareness, whatever you do, becomes imbued with a sense of quality, care, and love. The end will take care of itself. Don't get attached to the outcome. It will be whatever it will be.

Life is found underneath your life's situation. While everything is honored, nothing matters. Form comes and goes, but you become aware of the eternal underneath the form. You know nothing can threaten you.

NOTHING REAL CAN BE THREATENED, NOTHING UNREAL EXISTS – HEREIN LIES THE PEACE OF GOD
A Course in Miracles

Chapter Eight

LOVE IS ALL THERE IS

God is omnipotent, omniscient and omnipresent.

Basic truths:

1. There is only one.
2. Consciousness reflects.
3. The Universe is an illusion.
4. There is no separation.

Human beings and the universe appear to be either expanding or contracting. The main word in that sentence is "appear". In ultimate reality there is no contraction or expansion because there is only one. There is no enlightenment in ultimate reality because all is known as one. Enlightenment being the highest level of consciousness attainable, is an illusion because levels and states are made up and therefore only apparent.

We are dealing here with apparent reality because absolute reality is not comprehensible to the contracted mind. Consciousness in apparent reality is mostly contracted to totally asleep. Apparent reality translates into either "space or mass consciousness", depending on the level of reality one thinks one understands. Enlightenment comes from awareness at either level, be it expanded or contracted.

Space Consciousness

Space consciousness is the expanded (enlightened) state in apparent reality. In fact, all entities are in a one space consciousness but aren't aware of it. The process of "waking up" brings on the awareness of the expanded state. Space consciousness is the ultimate reality for all beings in separation. It evolves out of the dark state called mass consciousness.

We experience expanded consciousness as awareness, comprehension and understanding. A completely expanded individual has a feeling of total awareness or being one with all life. Total awareness means no resistance to any vibration or interaction of another being. It is timeless bliss, with unlimited consciousness, perception and feeling.

Mass Consciousness

Mass is the state of being contracted. It is the state of being unconscious. It is the darkest (without light) state of consciousness possible.

To the degree a person is contracted (unconscious) he is able or unable to be in the same space with others. Contraction is felt as fear, pain, ignorance, hatred, evil etc. At the extreme one feels insane which is defined as resisting everyone and everything, of being unable to chose the content of his consciousness. This is Hell.

The only way out of Hell (mass mind or contracted consciousness) is through consciousness expansion, which is the elimination of resistance to what one thinks, sees or feels. Resistance holds one to lower consciousness and is liberated only by love.

Energy

Energy is the vehicle for consciousness expansion. At the mid point between space and mass consciousness a person is logical and predictable. It is the "point" at which the ego begins to subside and one is able to enter the higher levels of awareness. It is what Dr. David

Hawkins calls the level 200, point of truth and integrity. See David Hawkins Scale of Consciousness in Chapter 6.

Energy is predictable and automatic. Space consciousness energy is high and vibrating rapidly with a sense of freedom. Mass consciousness on the other hand is characterized by low energy, vibrating more slowly with a growing feeling of compulsion and disorder.

The universe is full of both high and low energy vibrations which give rise to a variety of feelings, ideas and perceptions. The goal is to isolate some basic attitudes that will recover awareness and lead to freedom from the matrix.

There is nobody here but us chickens!

The entire universe is made up of beings like ourselves. Every particle in every atom is a being. Every molecule or cell is a universe of beings. Energy is the vibrating essence of the universe.

Mass is convertible into energy and energy is convertible into space and vice versa. Consciousness is a two way street. It is our withdrawal from awareness that makes us see our brothers and sisters as less than they truly are. In truth we are equal and are free to do anything we want to do within the laws of being equals. And the first law is...

Love

True Love is the result of being in a state of higher consciousness. If you are not in the same state of higher consciousness with other beings you are not in love. You are in loves opposite, which is fear. One's place in the universe is directly proportional to whether one has expanded in love or withdrawn from it. Pain and suffering are a result of spacing out love. Healing is the result of being in love.

Love is ultimately all there is. You are who you are and where you find yourself in the universe in direct proportion to your willingness or resistance to love. The kind of brain and body you have, your family and society, your date of birth and many other things are determined by your acceptance of love. No one did anything to you. You do it to yourself. There is no injustice. There are no secrets, nothing is lost, nothing is forgotten, all is included and no one is abandoned, not in love and love is all there is. The opposite of love is fear, which is the ego's domain. The body's eyes see everything that love is not.

All you need do is this:

Remind yourself to give full, permissive, loving attention to absolutely anything that you see in your mind, in your environment, and in other people. Consciousness expansion is available to every being in the universe all the time. It is the way home. A willing awareness will take you to heaven; a loving attitude will make you free. Nothing else controls your fate. Nothing else matters because ultimately there is no matter.

The Watcher

Whatever you are doing, love yourself for doing it. Whatever you are thinking, love yourself for thinking it. Love is the only "dimension" that needs consideration. The more in love you become, whether expressed or not, the more conscious you become. Waking up is a result of falling in love. Awareness is a result of falling in love. Be willing, be on the watch, do not judge and extend forgiveness (correction). See the Christ in yourself and in your brother. Be vigilant. Wake up. Go home. Heaven waits for you.

Don't worry about worse or better spiritual conditions. They take care of themselves in proportion to your waking up or not waking up to love. On some level everyone knows that they are getting exactly what they deserve. Your consciousness and your circumstances are directly proportion to your awareness that love is the only truth and nothing else is. Are you aware of this? If not become aware of it.

Your choice is always the same: to expand your awareness or contract it. If you resist what love has to offer you get the illusion of the world you see. We deserve what love has to offer which is everything that the world isn't. Acceptance is the key. The willingness to accept love will transform everything. It's in everyone and everything right now. It only needs to be accepted. It is accepted through recognition and extended through awareness. Expanded awareness is a result of loving yourself and others as yourself. Darkness is not the absence of light. It is the absence of love.

The rules of love are effective whether one agrees with them or not, whether one is conscious of them or not, whether one discusses them or not. Remember, love is a space concept not a mass concept. It needs not words or books only consciousness to activate it. Consciousness and love expand one another. Your choice is the trigger, which begins the process of waking up to love.

As you wake up, you wake up those that appear to be separate from you. When you become fully awake you realize there never was anyone or anything separate from you to wake up to. Waking up means it was all a dream to begin with. In ultimate reality there is nothing to wake up from.

The only reason you would not want to wake up is that you somehow enjoy the pain and suffering (ego version) of the illusory, physical world. Maybe you see yourself in the "game of life" and you really enjoy playing the game?

This is the definition of addiction. In truth there is nothing to correct because there is no love in illusion. Do not get attracted to the counterfeit reality.

A dream is an illusion. How would you correct an illusion? The same way you correct a dream. You wake up! Your ego's version of correcting the illusion is creating another illusion. The way you unmask the illusion is not by denying it but by extending love. There is nothing to do here but to wake up, extend Christ vision and go home. There is nothing in the universe that needs correcting. Everything is perfect the way it is now.

Enlightenment

There is nothing you need "to do" to be enlightened. Enlightenment is any experience of expanding our consciousness beyond its present limits. Be open-minded. Enlightenment is the process of expanding not arriving. It is limitless. It carries the seeds of positive and negative. Observe and move on. Be in love. Don't resist. Non-resistance allows us to rise above mass consciousness and all paradoxes. Just watch whatever comes into your life. Love it, love yourself even if you disliking it and move on. Remember, what you resist, persists. The more you open your consciousness, the fewer unpleasant events intrude themselves into your awareness.

Love as much as you can from wherever you are. This applies to everything and everyone, even if you find yourself hating something or someone. Remember, you are not your body or your circumstances. Say out loud, "I love myself for hating this" and simply move on, don't resist. Resist not evil least you give it a reality. Resistance is a seduction to make real that, which is not real.

Start loving by loving yourself. Love everything even your negative feelings, your boredom, dullness and despair. Learn to love yourself — all of yourself. When you learn to love your "self" you are in truth expanding love into many other beings because you and your brother are one. Loving yourself is loving your brother and by doing so the entire world is lifted.

Time

Our concepts, feelings and limited relations have beginnings and endings in time, but we do not. On the space level, when we are completely expanded, time is always NOW. On the level of mass mind time is always past.

The awareness of the passage of time takes no time, because there is no time in it. Just like the awareness of insanity is not insane or the awareness of confusion is not confused. The greater your awareness the more meaningless is time.

Time is a measurement of compulsive repetitions and interactions on the mass level. The more expanded one becomes the less compulsive and therefore the more subjective time becomes until it disappears. Expansion is directly proportional to love. The more you love the faster you vibrate, the less you need to control anything or measure it. As you become more enlightened you become less afraid of change and variety. You experience everything deeper and more lovingly.

Time is a requirement of the lower vibration and mass mind. When you are aware that you are one with all that is, there is no need for time or control. When you are asleep the reverse is true. When you feel separated and in the mass mind, your need for control increases and likewise your requirement to measure everything. Time is a function in mass not light. Time makes perception seem real and everything in mass is perception. There is nothing real in it. What you project has a linear quality that requires an element of time to register. Projection and perception can only occur in the mass mind not in space. Expanded beings are beyond time.

Linear Reality

Cause and effect, karma and reincarnation are all linear concepts and only time makes them real. Linear is limited by time and is therefore an issue of mass not space. Time concepts require measurement and are therefore not ultimately true.

Measurement at best is relative. Liberation from repetition and measurement is only possible through expansion, which is love. Separation, which is resistance to oneness, is a product of mass consciousness and brings on fear. Remember, "what you resist persists, what you look at disappears". Resisting is mass while looking is expansion. Resistance is in the past while observing is now. Hell is linear. Heaven is non-linear. You leave hell and go to heaven by entering the now.

Look upon the world, don't resist it, don't measure what is not real and watch it disappear. The less you love what appears to be unreal the higher your vibration becomes and the reliance on time is no longer necessary. Judgment makes resistance and time real or seemingly so. Give nothing that can be defined (judged) permanence. If it can be defined it is occurring in time and is therefore not real. The more you observe without attachment the more you rise in vibration, escape time and enter space. From space it is a short hop to heaven.

Time is suspended in the NOW. Completely stop thinking for a moment and you're there. Try it! See for yourself?

Without love you will experience more conflict, mass and pain. In ego, love's opposite, you are vibrating slowly and everything only seems to be moving fast therefore requiring the need for control and time. In love you expand and your life improves because your vibration increases and outer things slow down. When you're in love time is no longer important.

It all requires love. Love everything and everyone. Don't leave anything out. When you learn to love hell, you will be in heaven.

Ignore the sin and love the sinner

Remember that we live in a world of appearances. Nothing is true in mass consciousness because you see but darkly. Your attention (what you look at) is always life giving. When extending Christ vision, extend it everywhere and to everyone. Does the person you are addressing appear high or low? Either way do not judge, just extend. What you have to offer is love, nothing more (there isn't any more) and nothing less. Love is not ego. It doesn't require discussion or debate. Remember all beings are equal. They can only "appear" to be otherwise. There is a huge difference between awareness and appearance. Appearance is the opposite of awareness.

Withdrawing your awareness from expansion and keeping your attention on contraction is what got you into hell to begin with. To escape the world (hell), reverse the process. Do not believe in fear; believe in love (expansion). The way out is simple: Do not resist!

Reality

All beings participating in the universe are real. That would be you and I, the particles in the atoms, and all sub atomic reality. All are real, all are equal, all are of one thing. The relationships, groupings and massing are illusory.

The paradox is that all illusions come from what is real. It is but a reflection not a reality. The issue is one of consciousness. The lower the consciousness the denser the world appears. The higher the consciousness the lighter the world appears. They are both real. Consciousness makes the difference. Denying one in favor of the other is missing the point.

We don't need facts to be wise and loving. Different sets of facts are real at different vibration levels. The truth is the same for everyone; the facts are always a little different for everyone. If we use the physical plane to deny higher reality, we are deluded and vice versa. We cannot rise above the physical plane by denying its reality. We must love it and affirm the reality of the beings that form it.

Meditation will take you to a "place" that feels like there is no permanence in the world but once you come back you are faced with mass level reality. This experience is telling you that you exist on many dimensions at the same time. There is no this or that, but there is "a" this and that. As your awareness opens up you can choose the level of consciousness you want. The facts on one level will not work on another. Is it any wonder we all see thing differently?

To change your mind requires your agreement. No one will change unless they agree to change. You cannot help or hurt others without their agreement and no one can help or hurt you as well.

You will change when you are ready to change and so it is for everyone. Change will present itself when you no longer require your current understanding and want to move on. It may not occur to you in a lifetime and then again it may occur to you in every lifetime. You are free to be anywhere you want to be both in the world and beyond the world. You are capable of being in any time or vibration you choose.

Regardless of how trapped you feel, how weighted down by one day after the other, your fundamental freedom is not affected. You can choose or not choose in any moment. In any case you are not alone. There are many beings aware of you at all times, loving you, ready to make you feel it whenever you are ready to open up to it, taking care to see that you don't get in too deep, encouraging you to love yourself. There are infinite universes for you to be in. The question is "what do you want?" Once you know then go there. You have helpers all along the way.

Enlightenment doesn't care how you get there.

Once you become aware that there is a higher path and infinite realities you will want to explore them. The desire for truth is enlightenment itself. Once you go there you will want to share it. Wouldn't it be great if everyone were in love?

There are many paths to enlightenment but there is one path that is available to everyone all the time: LOVE. Love is beyond reason and you must go beyond reason to be enlightened. You have to be out of your mind to be in love!

No matter how confused or stupid or unloving other persons may appear to us, we have no right ever to assume that their consciousness is on a lower level than ours. They may be realizing far deeper dimensions of love. The very people we now see as vulgar, unenlightened, stupid, insane etc. – these people when we learn to love them and all our feelings about them, are our tickets to paradise. We must love them as they are and we must learn to love ourselves just as we are now. Otherwise we are denying the right to freedom, which is everyone's choice.

Chapter Nine

MEDITATION

"Prayer is when you are talking to God. Meditation is when God is talking to you!" ...Edgar Cayce

The English use of the word meditation comes from the Latin "*meditaito*", which translates into "contemplation". Meditation is a ritualized form of contemplation. Unlike "daydreaming" there is a purpose and a disappearing in meditation. It's not just spacing out. It is becoming one with all that is.

The earliest mediators were probably the shamans of the Stone Age hunting and gathering societies who used ecstatic states to heal, divine and prophesy. The Rig Veda, the earliest recorded literature of northern India (1,000 BCE) mentions meditative ecstasy but offers no formal technique.

The first written evidence of formalized meditation in India or China did not appear until the 4th or 5th century BCE in the *Tao The Ching*. Eastern forms of meditation are very sacred. The priests and adepts spend long hours in meditative states. This is their life's purpose.

Meditation is essential to transformation!

If you begin to get it that this earth is not a real place, you will also begin to question what is real. This was my experience. Not that I am transformed but I am "waking up" which is essential to transformation.

Remember in the Matrix Movie how long it took Neo to get it that he was indeed the "One?" Although he made the commitment (the red pill) he just couldn't believe (resistance) that he was the one. None of us can. At the end of the day we are all one because there is only one us. (You'll get that in Part III)

So, what are you doing with your "time"? Are you stuck in the Matrix or recognize you are stuck but cannot find a way out? That is why we have given ourselves "time". Why else would you have time? Nothing in the Matrix means anything. Are you focused on nothing? Meditation opens the door to freedom. It did for me and according to all the sages; you cannot do it any other way. So, which is it: freedom or bondage?

I would not suggest sky diving without a parachute nor would I suggest spiritual transformation (enlightenment) without meditation. Not that there is a requirement, it just does not work. You cannot get to heaven by reading a book. Enlightenment, awareness and transformation require commitment. It is strictly up to you. Remain on the wheel of samsara (suffering through separation) of liberate yourself by letting go of fear.

Meditation is not the whole way out but it will point the way. When I say "the way out" I mean this planet is not heaven or did you get that already? If it isn't heaven then it must be Hell. Wow! What a bummer. And what would hell be but separation from your source. The common language between you and heaven is meditation. No rhetoric, no ego; just you and your creator, your friend – YOU. Another big WOW!

Meditation is a broad term used for various practices done by an individual or group to calm the mind (suspend the ego) for the purpose of self-realization. Science would refer to this practice as non-specific or non-local even though results can be measured in the physical body and brain. The practice of meditation is a transportation device to transformation. You cannot get to your new destination any other way.

MEDITATION

My experience in doing drugs is that the drug experience is quite contemplative. When one is "stoned" the world looks different and your reactions to the world is different inside that artificial reality. The brain being altered with chemicals sees the world in a different construct; usually in the lower astral plane (primitive).

The brain, with or without chemical alteration, sees the world strictly from the ego's point of view. On the other hand the meditative state of mind is without ego because it is a silent, non-rhetorical state. It is a more pure state or awareness because only oxygen is introduced. Oxygen is how the Holy Spirit makes contact with all life forms. What one sees and experiences is so much clearer. Don't things seem clearer when you shut up, close your eyes and take a deep breath? Try it right now for a few minutes. See!

I have used the term transformation a few times in this writing and again in the last few paragraphs. While we will go more deeply into transformation in Part III, just what are we talking about? Transformation is the conscious and deliberate act of changing the deepest aspects of the human spirit through a self induced, divine act. Simply stated, meditation is your passport to absolute reality not relativity. Relativity is the Ego's job.

Meditation opens the door to the ultimate mysteries. You are no longer an "I"(ego). You become an abstraction devoid of ego. In the meditative state one withdraws from all "outside" objects and becomes immersed in an ocean of consciousness without barriers. I could say it is the dimension of truth except for the fact that there are no dimensions or truth in apparent reality. Meditation on the other hand is the state of pure being without limitation or definition. Would you call that the truth?

The gift of learning to meditate is the greatest gift you can give yourself in this lifetime. For it is through meditation that you undertake the journey to discover who you are and to find the stability and confidence you will need to live and die well. Meditation is the road to enlightenment. Meditation is an activity. Ultimately no activity is required. It is a trick you play on the ego to get you past the illusion.

The meditative state of mind is declared by the Yogis in Hinduism to be the highest state in which the mind exists. The first stage of meditative mind is called "samadhi" in which non-dual (no separation) consciousness is experienced. Samadhi can occur in or out of meditation once you achieve the understanding (knowing) of that state.

Meditation is mainly an Eastern form of prayer, devotion and practice. In the West, meditation found its mainstream roots through the social revolution of the 1960's and 70's, when many rebelled against traditional belief systems, especially Christianity's failure to provide spiritual or ethical guidance.

New Age meditation techniques were primarily rooted in "blanking out" usually aided with chanting. Mind altering drugs were also used and Harvard professors like Dr. Timothy Leary thought LSD was a Holy Sacrament. So did Dr. Richard Alpert (Ram Dass), a contemporary of Tim Leary at Harvard.

The one word that jumps out for me is "detachment". The mechanical mind is attached to everything. It seeks attachment for the purpose of identification. Our self-made reality demands we have reference points to measure where we are and who we are. We become so identified with those reference points that we become those points and forget who we really are.

Our jobs, marital status, kids, money, homes, cars, trips, organizations, etc. become our identity. This is the problem of attachment and false identification. Quantum physics would say there are no reference points and things do not exist as you think. You made them up, all of them. Why would you be attached to an illusion and call it security or happiness? Wouldn't you think it would be safer to place your values into something more permanent and real?

The only mechanism that will help you see through relativity with any clarity at all is the practice of meditation with the mindset that this is not a real place. Be the observer here and you cannot possibly be the victim. Again, it is all in your mind, which is the dominion of the Ego.

Pull the curtain off the trick. Meditation will take you past the sleeping dogs of judgment and non-forgiveness, which keeps the illusion alive.

If you have ever done psychedelics you can understand why Dr. Leary said what he said. These drugs expose the interrelatedness of all things. However, you cannot take heaven by storm. With drugs nothing is permanent. That should be enough of a clue but it's a trick. You think you have found heaven but you have lost your way.

So, you take more drugs or alcohol. Somehow it never dawns on you that this is a dead end? It takes a huge revelation to get it that chemicals are not the way in but the way out. In fact they are the way into greater darkness. It's amazing that any addict comes completely clean but miracles do happen.

Carlos Castaneda, considered by some to be the father of the New Age, wrote that the Toltec mystics of northern Sonora practiced "halting the interior dialogue", or quieting one's thoughts, as the key to meditation. His teacher, Don Juan Matus believed that the mind or the Ego was actually a "foreign installation" and was the chief cause of a person's misery and suffering. Doesn't sound like something a loving Father would do? Does it to you?

How do you stop the world and the siren's call? One can "see" the world only by stopping the self-absorption process. In other words the key to peace is getting out of your own way and giving yourself over to something "higher". Not getting higher!

My experience with meditation:

Posture is important but not critical, depending on one's level of understanding. It is my experience that the spine needs to be kept straight and upright. Often this is explained as a way of encouraging the circulation of the spiritual energy or life force (*Kundalini*). Personally, I cannot sit in the Lotus position because it is too uncomfortable. Therefore I sit in a chair, both feet flat on the floor and back straight. My hands are open and resting on the top of my lap. I close my eyes, listen to the outer or inner guide or music and take in deep breaths. Breathing is critical to meditation.

Focus on your breath the entire time. Focusing on the breath will suspend mind talk. Do this for 15 minutes and then comfortably listen to the music and breathe normally for 15 minutes.

Become a "watcher". This is also critical. There is nothing to do in meditation. But your mind (ego) will not go peacefully into the night. "Watching" and breath work are the keys to quieting your mind.

The key issue is attitude. Why are you doing this to begin with? What do you hope to gain? When I first started meditation, my mind was full of chatter. As a matter of fact it got worse. I would fidget and become restless. When I learned about focusing on my breath and the NOW, my mind (ego) gradually gave up. With practice you will move beyond the body and the mind. This is not an intellectual exercise. My breakthrough came from watching a guided meditation called "Brain Illumination" inspired by Her Holiness, Sai Maa. I highly recommend it.

A good friend (Thank you Russ) handed me a book one day about seven years ago. That book was <u>I AM THAT</u> which is over 500 pages of dialogue with Sri Nisargadatta Maharaj on non-duality. More on this in Part III.

There are over 100 concepts discussed in this reading. As you might have guessed, meditation is one of them. When asked by a student, "All teachers advise meditation. Please tell us what is the purpose of meditation"?

Maharaj:

We know the outer world of sensations and actions, but of our inner world of thoughts and feelings, we know very little. The primary purpose of meditation is to become conscious of and familiar with our inner life. The ultimate purpose is to reach the source of life and consciousness. When the unconscious mind awakens, one can hear, speak, see, feel and know without question. One becomes clear.

When the mind is quiet, we come to know ourselves as "pure witness". We withdraw from the experience and its experiencer and stand apart in pure awareness, which is between and beyond the two. The personality, based on self-identification, is imagining oneself to be something: "I am this, I am that". It will continue but only as a part of the objective world. Its identification with the witness snaps once you know the trick.

Meditation has no intrinsic goal, but the goal toward which it is applied is the transformation of consciousness; the tool of self-improvement and spiritual growth.

The ultimate goal of mystical meditation is union with the Absolute.

Secular View

Many in the West use a form of meditation to help improve a physical or mental condition, like health, creativity, self-esteem, success, or relationships. Spiritual meditation will not accomplish these goals, but may help people accomplish their own powers and abilities to do so. Science conforms that such practices as positive contemplation have positive linear effects. This Western version of an Eastern tradition is more aptly called contemplation rather than meditation.

Contemplation does not quiet the mind or effect bodily rest. Be careful with contemplation for it too is an ego game. The true objective of meditation is to go beyond thought to the absence of thought. This is concentration not contemplation.

Duality vs. Non-Duality

We will be spending more time on non-duality in the final section of this book. It is the key to transformation. Because of my experiences I have chosen two works: <u>A Course in Miracles and I AM THAT</u> to develop the story of transformation and the way home.

There are many paths home and many rituals to help you get there. Between the hundreds of books I have read and my expericnces, these two books and meditation have shortened the search. It has saved me time and time is short for all of us. Experience will be your best teacher. My experience leads me back to the silence where everything is clear and only love prevails.

The time we gave ourselves when we arrived on the planet is precious. If you knew time was all you had to find your way home or spend countless lifetimes in samsara would you continue wandering around in the earth carnival? When do you want to go home where there is no pain and sorrow for eternity? No one is going to do it for you. You are the salvation you have been waiting for.

We are entering a new age and with it comes a new responsibility. 2012 and the Aquarian Age are conceptually one in the same. If the Maya and several other civilizations are correct something fantastic is about to happen. Imagine how prepared you will be if you get started now. What if nothing happens? Think of how prepared you will be ultimately.

Nothing occurs "out there" because out there is in time. It all occurs "in you" which is out of time. Like I said in the beginning, if you are happy and satisfied with your life, if you are experiencing no pain or suffering then you are home – you are free. Indeed you are blessed. However, if something seems to be missing, it probably is. What is missing is you. You have failed to show up in your own life. But it is not too late.

All that is needed to go home is the desire to go and a little help. Practice meditation, stop your addiction to books, become a watcher and a guide will find you. It's only in the letting go that all is given.

Meditation will take you past the watchdogs at the gate to happiness. One dog is called judgment and the other non-forgiveness. Tame these two and the gate will open, I promise. Meditate upon it!

PART THREE

TRANSFORMATION

Chapter Ten

RESURRECTION IS OF THE MIND

Resurrection is not about the body.

Until you get this you cannot wake up. In fact getting this is your wake up call, your greatest revelation. Literalism misses the mark (sin) when it comes to understanding the mystery. Matter can only hold an idea, not "be" the idea. The human body is a carbon unit, which holds the "idea of Christ Vision" (not Jesus Christ). When the mind awakens to its true reality, the body will no longer be necessary. Matter cannot be preserved. It can be changed into another form of matter but it cannot be elevated into pure energy. Let go of the body and you let go of the world. Let go of the world and you are resurrected.

A Course in Miracles says on Page 1:

Nothing real can be threatened
Nothing unreal exists
Herein lies the peace of God.

This is how several hundred pages of material begin in a Course in Miracles. This reality statement makes a fundamental distinction between the real and the unreal. It also makes a distinction between knowledge and perception. Knowledge is truth and cannot be threatened because it is real. Nothing "real" can be threatened or altered or changed. Matter (the body) is obviously not real as it can grow old, get sick, die, decay and disappear. Doesn't sound too real to me?

Truth is unalterable, eternal and unambiguous. It may go unrecognized but it cannot be changed. Every mystery has to do with safeguarding the truth, which is enclosed in an enigma. The truth here is the body is not real but contains within it the real or the truth, which must be raised or liberated in order that the body knows itself for what it is.

It would be like bursting a balloon. The rubber matter houses the air. The balloon (the body, the perception) must disappear if its contents are to be revealed. Is that so hard to understand? Is anything in the material world permanent? No. This would mean that the human body is not permanent either. Right? It only holds an idea. It is not the idea itself.

It only makes sense that any statement about resurrection must apply to the mind not to the body. The Gnostics knew this, promoted this and were killed off by the Christians for saying so. Had we pursued the Gnostic path we would be at least a thousand years ahead of our primitive, superstitious beliefs in the 21st Century!

Truth has no beginning, middle or end. It's simply the truth. To know this (gnosis) is pure knowledge. To not know this presupposes perception. Perception would be the world of time, of changes, of beginnings and endings. Everything is subject to interpretation not fact. It is the world of birth and death, the world of scarcity, loss, suffering and pain. It is learned behavior not given truth. Perception operates on five senses, which are proven wrong by the very instrument of measurement that swears by their conclusions, the brain.

There can only be "one" truth (non-duality). Duality, on the other hand, means two or more. Truth's opposite (duality) is not a lie but the illusion of multiplicity. This is the "fractal" world of perception. Therefore we have two dual thought forms: Knowledge and Perception. In the realm of knowledge no thought or thing can exist separate from its source.

Once you separate a thing from its source it becomes something similar to the source (perception) but not exactly like the original.

Whatever it looks like, smells like, feels, tastes or sounds like (sense created) it is no longer the truth but a clever reflection or facsimile of the truth called an illusion. Therefore all sense-defined reality is an illusion brought on by perception.

What's real needs no defense because it cannot be threatened. No threat, no attack, no defense. On the other hand, if it is not real it will need to be defended because it is being attacked all the time. "Attack" here is a general term for "questioned or argued". The world of perception (the apparent world) if not real must be a dream. It is hard to escape a dream because your senses confirm every inch of it. So, how do you get out of the dream and back to the truth? The bad news is you cannot do it alone. The good news is you have Help. Now do not freak on me. Just stay tuned. Your helper is the Holy Spirit!

The Holy Spirit would be your alter Ego. It knows the truth and the illusion at the same time. It does not get caught up in the illusion but understands why you create them. It is the Holy Spirit's job to help us escape from the dream world by helping us reverse our thought process. It's the "flat world" idea.

The greatest tool you have to reverse your thinking is "Forgiveness" and the Holy Spirit is there to help you to remember how to use it. Forgiveness is your only way out of hell. Can it be that simple? Yes. Forgiveness is not a moral issue but a correction devise. The root meaning of forgive is *"to correct"*. If you are off course you need only to change course before you sail off the flat world. You need a "little willingness" and a "little help" and you will be on your way. How hard is that? Pretty hard when you consider you have been off course for many lifetimes.

"What about the world I see," you say? Well, what about it? " Well, it seems so real", you add. Great job I say. Now that you know it is not real how do you get out? Do you even want to get out? Better be clear about that first. Remember, the world is a reflection (illusion) of your own internal perception.

What is your dominant idea about yourself? What are your dreams and emotions? Remember always that what you are "projecting" inside yourself you are "perceiving"(as a man thinketh, in his heart, so is he). Here's how it works: First you look inside and decide what kind of world you want to see. Then you project that "image" onto the screen of your mind making it the truth as you see it.

Whatever we project onto the screen of the mind we believe to be the truth. A projection is not the truth but a projection. When you go to a movie, do you believe that what is on the screen is real? In the same respect what is on the screen of your mind is an illusion. How are you using perception now? What are you projecting onto your screen?

Let us say we are attempting to cover up some mistake or anger, possibly the feeling of not being loved or abandoned by a parent? This is your perception. You bought and paid for it. So, what do you suppose is your projection? What are you seeing (projecting) onto the world? Probably evil, destruction, malice, envy and despair. How could it be otherwise?

All this we must be willing to forgive or correct, not because we are "good" or "charitable" but because what we are seeing is not true. You have placed yourself in hell and want out because the suffering is too great. Only you can get yourself out of hell. What you resist persists. Hell is kept alive by resistance. Forgiveness sets you free. Stop looking at something that is not there. Stop re-creating hell like some gerbil in a cage spinning away to nowhere. Get off that treadmill by forgiving (correcting) your course.

Do you think you were created to suffer? Would a loving God want you to suffer? No. Suffering is your idea. That is what the crucifixion is all about. Forgiving yourself and others is like a crucifixion. "Father, forgive them for they know not what they do." You must go on that cross or nothing changes. Once crucified you can get off the cross forever.

"Sin" is defined as missing the mark. It is an old archery term from the Middle Ages. When an arrow was shot at a distant target (over 100 yards) you could not see if you hit the mark with the naked eye. If you missed the target the target judge would raise a flag to the left or right with the word "sin" on it meaning you missed the mark to the left or right, low or high. So, how does sin sound now? Again, you buy into things without fully knowing why or how.

Sin in A Course in Miracles is defined as "a lack of love", because love is ultimately all there is. Sin is a mistake to be corrected rather than an evil to be punished. There are no mistakes. There is ultimately nothing "out there" to be forgiven, only the perception/projection. Fix your projector and a new movie will play. The Holy Spirit knows this. He is waiting for you to show up. He cannot do it for you. He needs your help. Are you ready to do your part or do you like living in hell?

Do you believe in abundance or scarcity? Belief in abundance is a belief in love. Belief in scarcity is a belief in inadequacy, weakness and incompletion, which governs the worldview. It is an illusion. You will seek in others what you feel is missing in yourself. This is classic projection. We often "love" another because it is missing in ourselves. What we get back is not what we wanted because what we get back is colored by our own projection, which is primarily "needy". This is what passes for "love" in the dream world. If "love" is all there is then how can this happen? Because "love" in the world is a counterfeit.

Real love couldn't ask for anything. It is the little "I", the "self", who asks for anything because the little "I" doesn't know or trust in who it is. It looks into the illusion and then becomes upset when what is returned is not satisfying. The little "I" seeks approval, possessions and love in the world where they cannot exist. Hell knows not of these things. Hell can only reflect. You created the "self", God creates the "Self". The Self needs nothing. It is complete, safe, loved and loving. It seeks to share rather than to get; to extend rather than to project.

All relationships are "special" or "selfish". Either way, you lose. Why, because they keep you in bondage of not knowing who you really are. On the other hand the Holy Spirit, if asked to help, will convert all such "special" relationships into lessons of forgiveness and an awakening from the dream of separation. You must stop right here and ask yourself a question, what do I want?

Since perception is a body program what would be its opposite? Christ Vision! Again, not Jesus Christ, who exemplifies Christ Vision but the vision and determination to see through the glass even if darkly. Your senses, the Ego's game, seems to dim or block the Holy Spirit's attempt to wake you up. You cannot serve two masters. What shall it be the little "I" of the "Self", you decide. Would you rather hear the voice of Christ Vision or the pathetic little voice of the miserable ego?

Christ Vision is the Holy Spirit's gift, God's alternative to the illusion of separation and to the belief in the reality of sin, guilt and death. It is the one correction for all the errors of perception; the reconciliation of the seeming opposites on which the world is based. Its gracious light shows all things from a different point of view, reflecting the thought system that arises from knowledge and making return to love not only possible but inevitable. What is regarded as injustice, done to one by another, now becomes a "call for help". Sin, sickness, and attack are seen as misperceptions calling for remedy through gentleness and love. Defenses are laid down because there is no attack. Our brother's needs become our own as we are all on the same path home. Without us our brothers would be lost forever. Without them we could not find the way.

Forgiveness is unknown in heaven. However, in this world forgiveness is a necessary correction for the mistakes we think we have made. To offer forgiveness is the only way we can have it for ourselves. Forgiveness is the means by which we will remember. Through forgiveness the thinking of the world is reversed. The forgiven world becomes the gate of Heaven, because by its mercy we can at last forgive ourselves.

Hold not another in prison to guilt. Acknowledge Christ in all your brothers because in so doing we recognize His Presence in ourselves. Forgetting all our misperceptions, and with nothing from the past to hold us back, we can remember God. Beyond this, learning cannot go. When we are ready, God himself will take the final step in our return to Him.

What is Christ Vision?

This is your only purpose for being here: to see the world reflecting your own holiness. Everything seen by the body's eyes is a mistake for the body's eyes see only form (projection). Christ Vision or human judgment is always your choice. If you see the body, you have chosen judgment, which is the portal to hell. If you see the light you have chosen Vision which, is the portal to heaven. Vision reflects strength rather than weakness, unity rather than separation, innocence rather than guilt and love rather than fear. Christ Vision cannot see error but looks only upon holiness. Perceive your own holiness and you will perceive holiness in your brother.

Chapter Eleven

AWAKEN

Dr. Ken Wapnick introduced John Mundy to Dr. Helen Schucman and Dr. William Thetford in March 1975. During the next two years the three of them met on several occasions to discuss the information that was "coming through" Helen that would eventually be called <u>A Course in Miracles</u>. The Course was printed and released in 1981 after Helen's death and without any connection to her personally, which was in accordance with her wishes.

John Mundy was an ordained Methodist Minister in New York and from 1975-89 he tried to introduce his church to the Course. Finally the church put their dogmatic foot down and John was released from his lifetime work in June of 1989. He subsequently started Interfaith Fellowship in New York City in September 1989.

In his book, **Awakening To Your Own Call**, published in 1994, John provides a way of understanding some of the basic teachings of the Course. He points out that his book is no substitute for the Course but may be helpful to new students. John now travels the world teaching the Course.

Jon's book begins with looking at the ego and the ego's thought system and how the ego's system of defenses (primarily denial and projection) are used to protect itself. From here John takes up the practical application of the Course, which is healing through forgiveness. Forgiveness for this purpose is defined as: removing our projections of guilt onto others.

Next John's book takes a look at the metaphysics of miracles, which is closer to modern physics than theology. Finally the book arrives at looking at the "Happy Dream" – the dream of awakening – the realization that there is no love but God's and that we are able to awaken to our own call and return home again.

The Ego

The Course says we do not see anything (out there) as it is because our seeing is clouded by an ego-based thought system. The ego-based thought system operates in dualism, which requires judgment to hold it together. Without judgment it would collapse.

The ego operates on perception. The Course says, "Perception is interpretation". Therefore the ego is constantly interpreting or judging. Modern physics, Gestalt psychology and the Course are all saying that the perceiver and the perceived are the same, that there is no separation. Judgment is a by-product of separation. There is nothing to interpret or judge in non-duality. There is no subject/object relationship. No "you" independent of "it". These are all duality concepts.

Positionality only exists in the mind and is projected onto a seemingly separated world but the world you think you see is not separate from you. The world is not "out there". What you think you see is a reflection of the world inside.

The Course says there are two ways of seeing: that of the ego (outward) and that of the Holy Spirit (inward). Only one can be true. From the Course perspective true seeing means **"Christ Vision"** which is seeing as the Holy Spirit does which is either an expression of love or a call for love. In truth LOVE is all there is.

The ego was born out of an insane wish for separation and autonomy from God. The ego made time (past and future) and fears for its survival because it cannot comprehend eternity (Now). Not knowing eternity leads the ego to fear death because the ego believes you are a body and the body dies. The ego wants us to believe that illusions are real. Illusion is a result of guilt. A place, if you will, to hide from the truth of who you really are. While in reality there is nothing to be guilty of, the ego has convinced us otherwise. The ego is never satisfied with who you are. It whispers: "what do you wish to be someday" rather than "who are you today."

How did the ego happen?

The Course suggests that the ego came into being from a mad idea of "What if?" "What if?" suggested a separation from Source in order to experience "other". Because there can be no separation from Source, it apparently (appears) to happen in a trance or dream state. It happens in the mind and is projected onto the world. "What if?" is meaningful to the ego not the Holy Spirit.

"My meaningless thoughts are showing me a meaningless world." *A Course in Miracles*

Why do we continue to hold on to this meaningless mad idea of separation? It's a two-edge sword. On the one hand it gives us a sense of power and authority over the world we think we see, and on the other a sense of guilt. The ego projects that you have the power to define, describe, decide, interpret, analyze, condemn, project and judge the world. At the same time it suggests you are guilty for doing it. You are damned either way. This is the ego's game in the dream of separation.

The mind makes up its own world. If it is made up, it cannot be true.

I am sure you have heard the expression "Does it "make sense?" That's the ego's job – to make sense of the world. How many senses are there? You are convinced there are five and everything must fit into that reference. How limited.

"You make the world and then adjust to it, and it to you." *A Course in Miracles*

Would this not be Hell? But remember. "I do this but to myself."

Heaven on the other hand would be a pre-separated world. A space where there is no distinction between subject and object, where there is no pain and no fear. It is a space of pure love. It is the mind of God. It is the a-priori condition.

So, what world do you see? A world of sorrow and sin (error), the ego's world, or a world that reflects healing, harmony and happiness, the Holy Spirit's world. One separates and one unifies. One is Hell and one is Heaven. The world is in fact how you see it because the world is in you NOT you in the world.

It is the purpose of the Course to help us with our sinfulness (our misunderstanding) and our specialness, which is our desire to be singled out from the rest of creation and given special favor, special treatment and special love. Our task is to be willing to look at things without attachment to the ego – in other words without judgment.

We are just asked to be willing to put our denial, our anger, our jealousy, our impatience and our judgment aside for a moment and just look at it. We undo guilt through looking at it and seeing it in the light of forgiveness. Not looking is a way of holding on. Forgiveness is the act of letting go. Go ahead look at it, that's when you get honest and that's when the Holy Spirit steps in. That's when you grow up.

"What you resist persists, what you look at disappears'

Vision

Physical sight is an ego perspective. At best physical sight is confined to a spectrum of limited possibility. A microscope, binocular or magnifying glass will let us see what couldn't be seen otherwise. It's all a matter of perspective but in any event physical sight is limited and relative. The ego is the orchestrator of relationships. The ego allows us to see the world the way we have made it up. The Course suggests we are forever confusing form with content. Form changes and is therefore temporary and ultimately holds no eternal value. It's not the form that natters but the content.

Vision is the opposite of sight. Vision is not of the eyes but of the spirit – The Holy Spirit. True vision is a matter of insight. Insight is an inward experience.

Seeing with the eyes creates the requirement to judge. True vision has nothing to do with judgment.

"Vision would not be necessary had judgment not been made."
A Course in Miracles

True vision is the opposite of judgment. True vision is non-dual. It sees things as they are. Judgment comes out of fear. Vision comes out of love.

"Judgment will always give you false direction, but vision shows you where to go." *A Course in Miracles*

Vision reflects a decision to accept rather than to judge. There is no analysis or interpretation in vision. True vision suspends analysis and interpretation. True vision requires no "justification". True vision is not dreaming. True vision is not dual.

"Vision is the means by which the Holy Spirit translates your nightmares into happy dreams."
A Course in Miracles

Nightmares are products of the ego. A nightmare is getting caught up in the distractions of the ego.

True vision is not wishful thinking, conjuring, hoping, or use of positive affirmations.

There is a great difference between magic and miracles. The world is not changed by magic. Magic is an illusion.

Basic Truths

In this world we think that it is in taking that we receive. But why is it that in getting what we think will make us happy we often feel something is still missing? We are unsatisfied because we attained only a small part of this world. We did not attain Heaven. It is not in taking that we get anything. The truth is it is only in giving that we receive.

In this world we think that by making judgments we are justified. Judgment is a reason and logic mechanism of the ego, which begs to "figure it out". Ego propositions or ego arguments have no end to them. There is no solution possible, only judgment. We don't come to the truth by figuring it out. We come to the truth by becoming receptive to the Voice of the Holy Spirit. It is an inner trip. The truth is it is only as we suspend judgment that we have an opportunity for clarity.

In this world we think we are bodies. The cosmetic industry, the medical industry and the clothing industry are multi billion dollar industries that lend proof that we believe we are bodies. This fascination with the body keeps us from vision and mesmerized by physical sight. The emphasis here is on the physical not the eternal.

The body is a tool for learning and experiences, not an idol of distraction. We need the body for the purpose of waking up to awareness, not falling further asleep in ego-centered unconsciousness. The world is a classroom. You need a body to participate in the classroom. Giving up the body would be like dropping out of class. You need the body as long as there are lessons to be learned, as long as waking up is a goal. Just don't get lost in the process of having a body to do the work of awareness.

The truth is we are not our bodies.

In this world we think we can make ourselves right and in righteous indignation withhold our forgiveness.

The truth is we experience love only by extending forgiveness.

In this world we think of everything in terms of the past and future. How can we see clearly when we see the past where guilt, regret, nostalgia, and remorse cloud being here now? Jesus said, "Let the dead bury the dead". We cannot see clearly when our minds are preoccupied with what's dead (past).

The truth is there is only NOW – this holy instance.
"I see only the past" *A Course in Miracles*

The purpose of the Course is not to help make this world a more loving place but to help us look at this world in a more loving way. By doing this we bring this world to healing and to love.

Christ Vision

When we see things as they really are, without denial, projection, judgment, or condemnation, we begin to truly see.

**"See through the vision that is given you,
for through Christ Vision He beholds Himself.
And seeing what He is, He knows His Father"**
A Course in Miracles

Christ Vision sees the Kingdom of Heaven reflected upon the earth – right now, right here. Jesus said, "The Kingdom of Heaven is spread out upon the earth yet you do not have eyes to see".

Heaven is not going to come someday. It is not here of there. Heaven already is for those who see it. It is seen through Christ Vision, which is yours through the Holy Spirit.

Christ Vision comes as we look upon someone or some situation we might have judged before and let it be what it is. Christ Vision is an experience of peace.

It is possible to see a place where anger finds no home, where hurts are healed, a place that looks very much like Heaven. It is possible to see a place where loss is impossible, where love endures forever, where hatred cannot exist, and vengeance has no meaning.

A Footnote

Consciousness is not apart from the ego. i.e. consciousness and unconsciousness (opposites) are a part of the ego's thought system in duality. I believe that "what if?" is the metaphysical version of the "Big Bang". I believe consciousness is an evolutionary process. We are just now at the place where we can ask the questions and look for the answers. Consciousness is telling us to look inside. That would have been impossible prior to this stage of evolution.

The very thing that keeps us in darkness is now coming to light. Consciousness awareness is bringing us home to knowing who I am (the Son of God). With the Holy Spirit's help I am using the ego's thought system to bring me home.

Mass or dense consciousness has come a long way from "What if?" We are just now at a place where we can question, "What happened?" As mass consciousness stirs from its long unconsciousness and opens its spiritual eyes it wants to know who and what it is. That's where we come in.

At this stage of evolution the process of waking up becomes accelerated and the mind stretches to know itself. We arrive at the threshold of conscious-awareness for the first time in evolution and for the first time in evolution look inward rather than outward. Survival is no longer the primary function, the atonement is. The at-one-ment is our only responsibility in consciousness.

For the first time we have a conscious opportunity of "oneness". It could not have happened until we were able to ask the question and entertain the answer. This opportunity was not possible until Now; could not have been possible until Now. We have just recently become conscious of Now. This is what the consciousness revolution is all about. This is the dawning of the new age.

So now comes the task of "becoming" this great opportunity. There have been pioneers who have helped us (Jesus, Buddha, Krishna and others) with this waking up and there are many more who continue this work. A Course in Miracles and its students are an important part of that process.)

Chapter Twelve

NONDUALITY

When I first heard the term "nonduality", I put it out of my mind because it seemed too complicated. It used terms (Eastern philosophy) I was unfamiliar with so resistance immediately set in. That was five years ago. Now it seems the most obvious. It has opened my eyes to ultimate reality.

Actually, everything I have been reading and experiencing for twenty years is of a nondual nature. I just had that initial resistance to the term itself. It is like everything else, if you "get it" you "get it" and if you don't you don't but when you do "get it" you just know! There is no right or wrong, just wow! Remember, it's all perception anyway. Let me tell you a little about nonduality, as I understand it. Don't resist because of the terminology. Open your mind and see where your heart goes.

Nondulism implies that things "appear" distinct while not being separate. That sounds like a bunch of double talk, right? That was my first reaction as well. Consider this, in absolute reality (truth) nothing can be separate. It is either true or it isn't. It must be whole to be true or else something is missing and therefore false. Truth is whole. Truth is one. If separation were real, change would be possible. If change were possible nothing could be counted on from instant to instant.

Dual gives rise to judgment and with judgment you have ego and with ego you have the world as you see it. Where judgment exists differences are sure to follow. The word "dual" comes from the Latin *"duo"* meaning two and in English from the translation of the Sanskrit. The term can refer to a belief, condition, theory, practice or quality. Simply stated, there cannot be two of anything there can only be one. One what, is the question? One truth is the answer. Is not that what you really want?

Advaita is a Hindu monistic system of thought. The term refers to the identity of the Self and the Whole. The term is both a concept and a school of thought in Hindu philosophy called the Vedanta. Basically, that school of thought says that God (Brahman) is the only truth, the world is an illusion, and there is ultimately no difference between God and the individual Self.

Advaita Vedanta requires anyone seeking to study oneness to do so from a Guru (teacher).

The Guru must have two qualities:

1. Must be learned in the Vedic scriptures.
2. Must be established in God (Brahman) meaning he/she must have "realized" the oneness of Brahman in everything and in himself.

The seeker must serve the Guru and submit questions with all humility in order to remove all doubts. By doing so, advaita says the seeker will attain "moksha" (Self Realization) which is liberation from the cycle of birth and death.

The Seeker needs to have four qualities:

1. The ability to discriminate between the eternal substance (Brahman) and the substance that is in transition (maya).
2. Renounce enjoyment of objects in this or any other world, even heaven.
3. Concentrate on meditation.

4. The firm conviction that the nature of the world is misery and an intense longing for release from the cycles of birth and death.

This is obviously not a Western tradition but you can see from the requirements that the study is taken quite seriously. Advaita is a discipline of silence. While I am not fully committed, I continue to move in the direction of silence. The more I move the clearer all becomes.

There is no separation between "cause " and "effect" in advaita. You cannot have one without the other therefore they are joined. There is only Brahman, the One, the whole, the only reality. Other than Brahman, everything else, including the universe, material objects and individuals are false. Quantum physics is suggesting the same thing when it says there is no sub atomic reality.

Brahman is often described as the infinite, omnipresent, omnipotent, omniscient, incorporeal, impersonal, transcendent reality. Sometimes you will hear Him/It described as "neti neti" meaning "not this, not this" because it cannot be described as this or that. The supreme must remain nameless.

Due to ignorance, the Brahman is visible as the material world and its objects. The actual Brahman is formless and without any attribute. It is at best "Sat" (Infinite Truth), "Chit" (Infinite Consciousness) "Ananda"(Infinite Bliss). He/It is free from any kind of differences because there is nobody in reality but Him/It.

Examples of dualism include self/other, mind/body, male/female, good/evil, active/passive, dualism/nondualism etc. Nondualism can only be accessed as a belief, theory, condition, practice or tradition. A nondual philosophy maintains that there is no fundamental distinction between mind and matter, and the entire perceptive world is an illusion. Most Eastern traditions state that the true nature of reality is nondualistic.

The Newtonian, Cartesian method (linear, cause and effect) in the West holds just the opposite. It has not been until the 20th Century that science (Einstein) is beginning to embrace the Eastern philosophical imperative. At the end of the day Western science may arrive where Eastern philosophy began some 5,000 years ago.

To understand nondualism as a practice in self-inquiry, I look to the teachings of Ramana Maharshi and Sri Nisargadatta Maharaj. What these two sages have to say is what most of the writers in the New Age in the West are saying in different ways. If you read between the lines, every author referenced in this book is saying God is One and there isn't anything else. Does that sound like Eastern nondualism to you? It does to me and it does to quantum physics.

The philosophical concept of "monism" is similar to nondualism, both hold to the nonexistence of any other than One God. Monism is an outgrowth of nondual thinking. However the Western version of nonduality stops with the development of Judeo/Christian philosophy as God has many attributes that are interestingly like those of His creator, man. Western traditions demand opposing forces (resistance) and are therefore inconsistent with nonduality. Mechanics is extremely dual and therefore totally judgmental. On the other hand let us take a look at what one of India's great sages says about your nature and therefore the nature of God:

Ramana Maharshi

Who Am I?

The gross body, which is composed of the seven humors <u>you are not</u>.

The five cognitive sense organs of hearing, touch, sight, taste and smell which apprehend their respective objects of sound, touch, color, taste, and odor, <u>you are not</u>.

The five cognitive sense organs of speech, locomotion, grasping, excretion and procreation, which have their respective functions of speaking, moving, grasping, excreting and enjoying <u>you are not</u>.

The five vitals, which perform the five functions of breathing <u>you are not.</u>

The mind, which thinks <u>you are not</u>.

If none of these then who am I?

After negating all of the above as neti neti (not this, not this) <u>Awareness alone remains</u> – That I Am.

What is Awareness?

The nature of Awareness is Sat – Chit – Ananda (Existence – Consciousness-Bliss)

When will the realization of Self be gained?

When the world has been removed (objects), there will be the realization of the Self, which is the seer.

Will there not be realization of the Self even while the world is there?

No.

Why?

The seer and the object seen are like the rope and the snake. Just as the knowledge of the rope will not arise until the false knowledge of the snake goes, so the realization of the Self cannot arise if the world too is perceived.

When will the world be removed?

Only when the mind, which caused the world, is quiet will the world disappear.

What is the nature of the mind?

It is the wondrous power residing in the Self. It causes all thoughts to arise. Apart from thoughts there is no mind. Therefore thought is the nature of mind. Apart from thoughts, there is no independent entity called the world. In deep sleep there are no thoughts, and there is no world. In waking and dreaming there are thoughts and there is a world. The mind projects the world out of itself. When the mind is in control, the Self disappears. When the Self is present the world disappears. The mind always exists only in dependence on something gross and it cannot stay alone. That is why the mind is called the subtle body.

What is the path of inquiry for understanding the nature of the mind?

That which arises as "I" in the body is the mind. If one inquires as to where in the body the thought "I" arises first, one would discover that it is in the heart. That is the place of the mind's origin. Of all the thoughts that arise in the mind, the "I" thought is the first. Everything else comes after. Without the first there is never a second or third.

How will the mind become quiet?

By the inquiry, "Who am I?" The thought who am I will destroy all other thoughts. Then, there will be Self-realization.

What is meant by Self-realization?

When other thoughts arise, one should not pursue them, but should inquire: " To whom do these thoughts arise?" It matters not how many thoughts arise. It only matters as to whom these thoughts have arisen. Is the answer to me? There is no me. The me is the second and third thought not the first.

It takes practice to be single minded. When the mind stays in the heart the world disappears. When the subtle (physical) body goes out through the brain, it creates a world. Stay in the heart and ego cannot arise. The ego, the world and all illusion arise with the "me". When the mind stays in the heart, the "I", the source of all thoughts will go, and the Self, which ever exists, will shine.

A Course in Miracles is an expression of nondualism that is independent of any religious denomination. The Course is quite clear that God did not create the physical world or universe or anything physical including you or me. The Course parts company with the Bible on page 1 word 1. In the Course, God is absolute reality. There is nothing beyond the "absolute". End of discussion.

Gary Renard in The Disappearance of the Universe states that, " We don't exist in an individual way – not on any level. There is no separated or individual soul. There is no Atman (soul) as the Hindus call it except as a mistake in the mind. There is only God." There is a statement in Chapter 14 of the Course that says, "The first in time means nothing, but the first in eternity is God the Father, Who is both First and One. Beyond the First there is no other, for there is no order, no second or third, and nothing but the First.

Both the Course in Miracles and Indian advaita agree on many points. What God did not create does not exist. The world you see has nothing to do with reality. It is of your imagination.

Chapter Thirteen

EAST AND WEST

THE EAST

Hinduism

Hinduism is often referred to the oldest living religion. Hinduism is formed of diverse traditions and has no single founder. It is the world's third largest religion after Christianity and Islam with approximately one billion adherents. Approximately 900 million live in India. Hindu philosophy is recorded in a vast body of texts of which the "Vedas" and the "Upanishads" are the foremost in authority, importance and antiquity. Contemporary Hinduism is predominantly monotheistic. But Hindu tradition includes aspects that can be interpreted as pantheistic, polytheistic and even atheistic. Other notable characteristics include a belief in reincarnation and karma, as well as dharma, which means "personal duty".

Hinduism does not have a system of beliefs encoded in a declaration of faith or creed like Christianity and Islam. The term itself encompasses many ancient religious traditions going back over 7,500 years. "Hindu" was an English term meaning "Indian pagan" in the 17th century, but the word Hinduism, denoting a world religion did not come into being until the 19th century.

The earliest evidence for prehistoric religion in India dates back to the late Neolithic period (5,500 –2,600 BCE.). The beliefs and practices or the pre-classical era (1,500 –500 BCE.) are called the historical Vedic period. Modern Hinduism grew out of the Vedas dated from 1,700 BCE. The oldest Vedic tradition exhibits strong similarities to Zoroastrianism and other Indo-European religions.

Rather than a religion in the classical sense, Hinduism is a religious tradition. It is said that Hinduism can only be experienced not defined. There are 5 prominent themes in the Hindu belief:

1. Dharma – dealing with ethics or duty.

2. Samsara – dealing with cycles of birth, life, death and rebirth.

3. Karma – dealing with action and subsequent reaction.

4. Moksha – Dealing with the liberation from samsara

5. Yoga – dealing with paths and practices.

Most Hindus believe that the spirit or soul called the "Atman" is eternal. This soul is indistinct from Brahman, the supreme spirit. This eternal connection means there is no separation from the infinite. God is one. This is the nondual philosophy called "Advaita." The Upanishads hold that whoever becomes fully aware of the atman as the innermost core of one's self, realizes an identity with Brahman and thereby reaches moksha (liberation and freedom).

There are dualistic Hindu schools of thought that understand Brahman as having personalities much like the Jewish God and the soul "atman" is awarded or punished according to how one acts in the physical world. This form of Hinduism subscribes to the polytheistic version of multiple Gods with multiple agendas.

In whatever ways a Hindu defines the goal of life, there are several methods (Yogas) that sages (teachers) have taught for reaching that goal. Paths that one can follow to achieve the spiritual goal of life include:

1. Bhakti Yoga – the path of love and devotion.

2. Karma Yoga – the path of right action.

3. Raja Yoga – the path of Meditation.

4. Jnana Yoga – the path of wisdom.

An individual may prefer one or several yogas, according to his or her inclination and understanding. Eventually all yogas lead to love and therefore Bhakti yoga is supreme.

The vast majority of Hindus engage in religious rituals on a daily basis. Most Hindus observe religious rituals at home. Hinduism has many festivals throughout the year. The festivals celebrate events from Hindu mythology, often coinciding with seasonal changes.

Hinduism is based on the accumulated treasury of spiritual laws discovered by different people in different times. These laws over time became scriptures, which were transmitted orally in verse form to aid memorization, for many centuries before they could be written down. Over centuries sages refined the teachings. Today the scriptures are not interpreted literally. More importance is attached to the ethics and metaphorical meanings derived from them.

Most sacred texts are in Sanskrit, which in most cases is not translatable as the language in which they were written because it has been lost in time. Sanskrit is found in two classes: Shurti and Smriti. The former (Shurti) refers to the Vedas, the earliest form of Hindu scripture, and reflect laws governing the spiritual world. The Vedas focus on rituals. The Upanishads focus on spiritual insight and philosophical teaching. The Smriti (memory) texts deal with epics of mythology.

Buddhism

Buddhism, as traditionally conceived, is a path of salvation attained through insight into the ultimate nature of reality. Salvation is not extended but earned. Buddhism encompasses a variety of traditions, beliefs, and practices largely based on the teachings of Siddhartha Gautama, commonly known as the Buddha meaning "the one who woke up" or became enlightened (bodhi).

It is believed Buddha was born of nobility in the city of Lumbini around the year 563 BCE. in modern day Nepal, India. And died at the age of 80 in Kushingar, India. He lived and taught in and around the northern Indian sub-continent. Buddha was an "awakened" teacher/philosopher, who shared his insights with average people to end suffering (disturbing thoughts bringing on unpleasant circumstances), achieve nirvana (balance) and end the endless cycle of suffering (Dukkha) and rebirth (Samsara). Buddha is credited with finding the "Middle Way" after years of denying his self.

The Middle Way or Path has many definitions:

1. The practice of non-extremism: a path of moderation away from the extremes of self-indulgence and self-mortification.

2. The middle ground between certain metaphysical views that things either do or do not exist, either being true.

3. An explanation or Nirvana (perfect enlightenment), a state wherein it becomes clear that all dualities are apparent and delusory.

4. The ultimate nature of all phenomenon is emptiness.

Impermanence in Buddhism is the key to understanding suffering. Impermanence expresses the Buddhist notion that all compounded or conditioned phenomena (things and experiences) are inconsistent, unsteady, and impermanent. Everything we experience through the five senses is made up of parts, and all existence is dependent and conditioned. Everything is in a state of flux, and is therefore changing. Things are constantly coming into being, and then ceasing to be. Nothing lasts.

Attachment to this impermanence is an illusion and can only arrive in suffering. According to this doctrine, human life embodies impermanence in the aging process, the cycle of rebirth, and in any experience of loss. Detachment is the way to nirvana and an end to all suffering and rebirth.

Islam

Islam is the world's largest religion with approximately two billion, primarily third world, adherents. Muhammad, Islam's prophet, was born in 570 CE. At age 40 Muhammad had a revelation that he was God's only true prophet and that Islam is the only true belief and must replace all other beliefs in the world.

Muhammad sees the Jewish and Christian traditions, as being the same and their God is a false God. Jesus was a prophet/teacher, not the Son of God. God has no son, but He does have one true prophet in Muhammad.

Allah is the one true God, which was a tribal god in Arabia for hundreds of years. Allah was a war god similar to Yahweh and El for the Jews. Allah is elevated to be the only God under Muhammad. Muhammad lead 82 attacks on his neighbors over 20 years to legitimize himself and his tribe, the Quresh. Muhammad gets his authority and orders directly from Allah. Everything is "revealed" to Muhammad. It was revealed for instance that the taking of slaves was acceptable and having four wives was acceptable for his tribe only. The Quresh became the dominant tribe by birth rate.

Islam means, "Surrender to God". Not just the tribes of Arabia but all mankind.

Jerusalem is considered Muslim holy ground because when Mohammad died his chariot touched down at the Dome of the Rock where He met Abraham and Jesus and they all decided Muhammad was the chosen prophet and that Jerusalem was holy Muslim ground because Abraham was not a Jew but a Muslim and Abraham is in reality the father of the Muslims not the Jews!

Abraham had two sons: Ishmael by Hagar an Egyptian slave woman and Issac by Abraham's wife Sarai or Sahah who conceived at the age of 90 !

The Myth - Because Sarah couldn't conceive when she was young Sarah suggested Hagar (Sarah's bondswoman – a slave) and in fact Hagar did conceive. By custom the baby would have been Sarah's anyway.

Hagar conceives and a son – Ishmael is born. Then all of a sudden Sarah gets pregnant and has a son – Issac. Sarah is jealous of Hagar and sends Hagar and Ishmael into the desert to die. The Jewish story is that Abraham's legitimate son would be the founder of God's chosen people – the Jews. That son would be Issac.

The Muslim story is that an "angel" (messenger in Greek) appeared to Hagar and Ishmael in the desert, saved their lives and promised them that Ishmael was God's favored son and would be the founder of "God's chosen people" which of course are the Muslims.

So, are the Muslims the bastard offspring of the illegitimate son of Abraham? According to Muhammad – yes, but it is God's (Allah's) Will and by the way, Abraham was Muslim and it was Ishmael who found favor with God at the "sacrifice" story not Issac.

Jesus was a considered a prophet, but not the Son of God and was never crucified as reported in the New Testament.

Qur'an - Is the written "Word of God" (620 CE.) It finally made it into print in the 10th Century. It is somewhat ambiguous as to who is talking, Muhammad or God. The book rambles in places and is quite incoherent in others. From the 7th to the 10th Centuries there were a number of changes to fit the occasion.

Holy War (Jihad) - This concept was born with Muhammad and states in that "you are either with God and his prophet or against them". War then becomes a holy instrument to fulfill this revelation. The Jihad is waged against the "unclean" or "infidels" who are those who will not bend to Islam.

Heaven is predetermined at birth.

Hell makes the Christian Hell look like a nursery school.

Judgment Day will come when the Muslims have conquered Jerusalem.

ISLAM is the fastest growing religion in the world today.

THE WEST

The term "Mystery" derives from the Latin "*mysterium*", and from the Greek "*musterion*" meaning "secret rite or doctrine." An individual who followed such a mystery was called a "*mystes*" or mystic, which literally translates as one who has been initiated. The ceremony for the initiate was called the "closed mouth and eyes" ceremony in ancient Greece and Rome. Only the "closed mouth and eyes initiates" would be exposed to the truth. These mysteries were copied from the ancient Egyptians.

The uninitiated, (the ignorant) were not allowed to know the inner workings of the cult (primarily astrology) and were kept in "the dark" (without the sun). This gave rise to a priesthood who dominated belief on every continent for thousands of years. If you expected to survive you had to go to the priesthood.

Mystery religions, sacred mysteries or simply mysteries were religious cults of the Greco-Roman world, participation in which was reserved to initiates. As far back as 2,500 BCE., the Egyptians had developed a priestly class and in fact were preparing initiates in inner temple rituals beginning with the first dynasty. All great civilizations including Western Christianity had a mystery teaching available to the select few. The few were normally selected from within the priesthood or from the aristocracy.

The main characterization of these religious groups is the secrecy associated with the particulars of the initiation and cult practice, which may not be revealed to outsiders. The most famous of the Greco-Roman initiation cults were the Eleusinian mysteries (1600 BCE.), which predated the Greek Dark Ages and lasted for over 2,000 years. This myth and its initiate practices were help all over the

Roman Empire until the formation of Christianity (400 CE.). Theodosius I closed all mystery sanctuaries by decree in 392 CE.

Most all mystery schools were formed around agriculture themes. The arrival of the Winter Solstice (after losing sun light for 6 months) is critical to all agrarian themes. With the arrival of more sun (later to be personified in the Son) there is hope for salvation. This is true from Egypt to Christianity and practiced on every continent of the earth in some form.

All the sun gods eventually become the "Sons of Gods." Julian the Apostate, a Gnostic priest and scholar, was initiated into three distinct mystery cults in the 4th century CE., notable the Mithraic Mysteries, which is the direct model for the Jesus story. In all these mystery schools, man's existence and his continued existence was based on astrology. The symbols of the cults manifested in either pure myth or the attachment of the myth to a human being.

Although Christianity at large was not a mystery religion it is based on the same mysteries (myths) entertained for centuries. The central mystery in all these schools, including Christianity, was the dying and resurrecting sun ("son"). His sacrifice on the cross (at the intersection of the winter and summer solstices and the spring and autumn equinoxes) insured a new spring, a new crop and a new harvest. These myths are a way for man to identify with God.

Salvation, resurrection and eternal life are the themes of all mystery schools including Christianity. If it had not been for the Emperor Constantine, and the establishment of "the one true church", we might still have mystery schools today. We do have mystery societies which emulates the ancient practices.

Justin Martyr, one of the Church's early fanatics, noted the parallels between all ancient mystery schools and Christianity and declared them to be heretical and a trick by the devil to circumvent the "one true church." Therefore, and on his order, all ancient mystery schools were put out of existence and their followers either Christianized of killed.

No competition, no argument.

Chapter Fourteen

TRANSFORMATION

Congratulations! You have reached the beginning. We have arrived at the beginning of your search for enlightenment. In Part I you went through the undoing of the status quo (belief). In Part II you considered the major issues you need to prepare for if you want to move into the awakening. I then gave you a few keys in Part III to help you understand what is necessary for the changing of your mind, which is Buddhism for salvation.

I have spent 30 years getting to what I am about to say next. A consciousness revolution is at hand. Are you prepared?

As I said early in this writing, you could have skipped reading this book and gone straight to <u>A Course in Miracles</u> or <u>I AM THAT</u>.

If you feel more comfortable with Christian based literature, <u>A Course In Miracles</u> may be for you. If you are not Christian <u>I AM THAT</u> could be your answer. Either way you will save yourself many lifetimes with either. Both works cuts to the chase and points the way.

I like both approaches because they are nondualistic, but I am really drawn to the Eastern approach because I have no theology. I suppose that makes me an a-theist. So be it.

Just saying that is liberating. Not to be tied to any creed or dogma is so freeing. That is what <u>I Am That</u> has done for me. It has freed me from further searching. No church, no dogma, no ideology. So, what is this I Am That all about and how does it fit with December 21, 2012?

Before we take a look at the teachings of Nisargadatta Maharaj I would like to say that to release oneself from the matrix, addictions, old patterns and ignorance one must first acknowledge that there is something to be released from.

There must be a surrendering. The only thing to be released from is the prison of your mind. Have you got it yet that there is nothing out there? There is no magic either. Magic is yet another misunderstanding to be eliminated because magic is an illusion. Giving up ignorance will be difficult for most readers because of comfort zones. Illusions are quite believable. Why do you suppose addictions persist?

You and only you give power to what you want to believe. Your beliefs are all made up. The undoing of that could take a lifetime or lifetimes or a few minutes depending on how attached you are to your beliefs. While going home is a choice it comes with a price. Very few of us, especially in the West, are willing to pay the price.

It's your little willingness that makes it possible. It's not like brain surgery. But then again...

Sri Nisargaddata Maharaj

There is a book and a video library entitled I AM THAT.

Maharaj is the teacher and the questioners are his students. I have been through this material several times which has led to some enlightening experiences. To me it is all about the experience, although in the end the experience must go as well. But, you must start somewhere if you are looking for self realization.

Read the book and remember that your Guru is ultimately you! Ask yourself: How far down the path of healing do I want to go? What am I willing to sacrifice to give up hell and return to heaven? After this final chapter you will need to go to work incorporating this material into your life if you truly want the healing. The healing is real for the sincere. To be healed (forgiven) you must make a commitment. Are you sick and tired or being sick and tired?

It would not hurt to find a teacher for the first part of your journey. Do you want to move on to the final chapter of your life, which is going home? Do you have that urgency? If not stop here because this chapter and the final step will end your existence, as you have known it. By the way, this is a good thing.

Do you get it yet that most of your problems stem from what you have been told? What are the words and thoughts that define you? All words and thoughts are abstractions. There is no reality in any of them! They have no meaning other than the meaning you give them. Where do these words and thoughts come from? It's all made up.

So, why do you spend your valuable life believing in nothing? The reason for most of us is we have been poorly taught. Be prepared to erase your tapes (programs) and start over. It's not as difficult as you may think. The reward is heaven. Remember Jesus suggesting that "The kingdom of heaven is where you are?" It may just be worth the effort.

Do you see that all your problems are your body's problems? Food, shelter, family, name, fame, security, happiness and survival. If you can come to understand and accept that you are not your body then you have no problems. The only thing you can know for sure is that you are. Focus on the I AM without adding anything to it.

If someone were to ask you the question, " Who are you?" How would you answer? You would probably start your answer with I am this or that. If asked who is the "I" you just referred to, you would not be able to answer because you do not know. Isn't it interesting that you have a definition for everything on Earth except for yourself? The I is the ego. What follows the "I" is made up. Stop making stuff up!

You might give some references to yourself but never be able to say for sure who you are. Why? Because the "I" is an invention, a reference point. The ego's domain is entirely made up and taken for granted. It is a dream with arms and legs. It is no more real than your dreams are real. This information may seem logical or it may seem illogical but you need to stay with the question and see where it takes you.

December 21, 2012 is an opportunity not a doomsday. If you start the path of self-realization today, by the time the calendar hits midnight on December 20th or sooner, you will get what the Mayans and others are saying. A new age is inevitable. The new age is a new consciousness. Can you imagine not being prepared for it?

The new age will be golden, which is the ancient term for enlightened.

Time is a way of defining who you are not. Soon there will be no more time to track what you are not. Who needs it? The old consciousness will not work in the new age. It's time to surrender to love. That is why the calendar ends. Don't you see it must end? We cannot continue to embrace desire and fear. The time has come to give up the illusions that govern your life. It's time to enter the Garden.

When your mind enters the "I AM" without definition and without verbalization, you are in the no-thing, no time zone. The trick is to stop attaching things to youself that do not exist. The matrix is kept alive by attaching concepts to the I Am like "I am a body with feelings, thoughts, ideas, possessions" etc. Escape the matrix. All of these "self" identifications are misleading. You are none of these. You can't even define them. These identifications create and maintain a "self", which is the antithesis of the "Self" and who you really are.

Because of these false identities you take yourself to be something you are not. You can only know who you are by knowing who you are not. This is a dichotomy. That is why you keep doing the same thing over and over again, lifetime after lifetime, expecting different results.

You think it is difficult to find yourself when it is just the opposite. Once you realize this you will stop the verbal "I Am" abuse and just simply go with "I Am." It will take practice to stop the "verbal" I Am in favor of the "silent" I Am. Practice is what you need. You have practiced the verbal version since the day you were born! Where has it gotten you? At the end of the day even the I Am must go but that's another story. You have enough to start with now.

Let go of the attachment to the unreal and the real will show up. Detachment is the clue. Remember, what the sage Jesus said, "What you resist, persists, what you look at disappears." Stop imagining yourself being or doing "this or that" and it will gradually dawn on you who you really are. Who you are is not in the "doer or the doing." The verbal I Am comes from your head where chemicals mix to form thinking (the mind). The mind is a product of chemical reactions. You are not your mind.

The non-verbal I Am comes from the heart. Anything coming from the brain is a needy chemical reaction telling you something is missing. That would be the verbal definition of Love. Love coming from the heart has no language, is powerful and makes all things loveable. Which one do you feel is fulfilling (full-feeling)?

All "definitions" point to the body and the mind. Neither the thing pointed to nor things pointed at have any permanency. Why would you worship them? Do you not see that this is idle (idol) worship? Once this addiction to "I am a body" idea ceases, you will revert to your natural state, which is Love. Just for a moment try to stop talking to your "self" and see how you feel. I think you get the message.

An old sage once said, "Between the banks of pain and pleasure the river of life flows. It is only when the mind refuses to flow with life, that it gets stuck on the banks." Getting stuck means refusing to flow with what comes and becoming identified with what's on the bank. Do not accept what comes but watch what comes without buying into it.

Remember, you are not what happens in your life or even whom it happens to, you are simply the observer of what happens, the witness. When something fearful happens and you go to the past, it is but poor memory and painful. Desire is in the future and equally painful. Both make the mind fearful and restless. Pain is of the body while suffering is of the mind.

Moments of pleasure are only gaps in the stream of pain. How can the mind ever be happy? It never can. On the other hand if you go to the future it is pure imagination because nothing ever happens in the future.

Mind divides and opposes. Only in escaping the mind can one find happiness. The mind creates the abyss but the heart crosses over it.

From what has been said so far it should be clear that you are neither your body nor your mind. You use both or abuse both but you are neither. The mind is a chemicalization going on in the brain. Because chemical reactions are continually changing, the mind can never be still. That is why it is hard to concentrate on anything for very long. That is why meditation is resisted initially until you can stop the chemical turbulence. Strive for silence. It is the best teacher.

Meditation is the only way to calm the mind. Remember, you are not your mind but you are consciousness. It is not the same as awareness, which allows for conscious to have a reality. You cannot overcome the mind or conquer the mind but you can shift your consciousness beyond the mind. You do this by refusing all thoughts but one: the heartfelt thought I Am. The mind will rebel in the beginning but will ultimately yield to the wonder of it. Once you are quiet, things begin to happen spontaneously and naturally. You begin to fall in love for the first time.

The world is but a reflection of your imagination. Whatever you want to see, you see. What you think you see happened before you even looked upon it. You think your pretty fast? You haven't even started yet. All your senses are just catching up to your projections. Everything you sense happened 99.9% of the time before you ever sensed it.

This brings up the conditions of "awareness and consciousness." Are they the same? No. Awareness is the a priori condition. It is the original state, without beginning, endless, uncaused, unsupported, without parts, and without change. Consciousness is a reflection from awareness. It forms a duality like looking in a mirror. There can be no consciousness without awareness, but there can be awareness without consciousness. Awareness is what happens in the silence.

Awareness is absolute; consciousness is relative. Consciousness is partial and changeful while awareness is total, changeless, calm and silent. It is the common matrix of every experience. There is awareness in every state of consciousness but not visa-versa. To go straight to awareness you must drop all definitions. Awareness is not of time or defining. Time exists in consciousness only. Time has no reality while awareness is absolute. Drop time and you are aware. You are home.

All the objects of consciousness form the universe. What is beyond consciousness and the universe is the supreme state of essence or supreme awareness. It is the state of utter stillness and silence. Whoever goes there, disappears. You can't "go" there by words or mind. Nothing the mind suggests does it justice. It is the nameless, no content, effortless, and spontaneous state, beyond being and not being. It is pure awareness.

Apparent Reality

There is nothing wrong with the world. What is wrong is the way you look at it. It is your imagination that misleads you. Imagination both creates the world and reflects it back to the perceiver. The world perceived is made up of consciousness. What is called matter is consciousness itself. You are the space in which the world has its beginning, turns and ceases to be. Cut off your imagination and attachment to the world and see what remains. Only awareness remains.

Projection/perception becomes so hypnotic that one begins to give importance to what is redundant. Gradually, like the frog in boiling water, you become attached to your perception. So what is real and what is an illusion? What can be counted on?

First, let go of your attachment to that which is subject to change and the real will show up. The real is love and comes from the heart not fabricated in the brain. Remember, the mind creates the abyss but the heart crosses it.

What is the difference between the person who realizes the truth and the ignorant person who embraces the illusion? The only difference is that the" self realized", person sees life as a succession of events without becoming attached to the outcome. The detached, self-realized person sees life as a passing parade. The attached person joins the parade and is pulled along by the illusion, lifetime after lifetime.

The way out is the way in. You have simply forgotten who you are. Re-member or re-join who you are and you are whole. Only a whole person knows who he is. Only a whole, re-membered person can go home.

The way back into the Garden of Eden is the Tree of Life. Life is non-dual. The goal is the I AM. You get back to the I Am and The Garden by refusing and rejecting all your attachments. While it will take some work you must give up the lie that this earth is a real place and that you are separate and alone in it.

Even the sense I AM is not continuous but only a pointer. It merely shows you where to look not what to look for. Once you have detached from what is false only the I AM remains and it too will disappear once verbalization has run its course. Once you have overcome the requirement of your ego to define your reality you are free to go home.

Your natural state is without definition. It may take a lifetime to discover who you are without definitions, but that's okay. Better this lifetime than the next or the next thousand! If you want to break the cycle of birth and death you will have to take the path of finding yourself sooner or later. That is why you are here in the first place.

The key to finding yourself is "earnestness." Earnestness means consistency. Time is not important. It is never too late to change if you are sincere. Finding out who you really are is not that complicated.

Your ego is simply causing you to forget. All that is required is to "remember" who you are. That doesn't sound so difficult or does it? Waking up is the solution. You can wake up if you really want to. You have help. It's called the Holy Spirit.

Death

Ultimately there is no death. Yes, there is a termination of the carbon unit ignorantly called death, but life is perpetual. It's the only game there is and it last for an eternity. There is no escaping life. Consciousness, the reflection of awareness, is likewise perpetual but requires a supporter. Life will always produce another supporter of consciousness. All bodies come with a knower and the new body will likewise have a knower but not the same knower from the last manifestation. Only memories remain from lifetime to lifetime.

There is a link between all knowers called the memory body or causal body. It is a record of all that was thought, wanted or done. Reincarnation is not about personality but about the memory body. Just remember that in death only the carbon unit disappears. Life does not cease. Consciousness does not cease. Life is never so alive until the burden of the body is lifted. Beyond life is ultimate reality, which is pure bliss. Bliss has no definition.

Reality

Experience is not real. Why? Because experience is of change and change is not real. Only constancy is real. Reality is not an event because it cannot be experienced. Reality is not perceivable in the same way as an event is perceivable. Events are projections in the field of time. Reality is beyond the field of time where perception/projection cannot go.

If you wait for an event to take place, for the coming of reality, you will wait forever because reality neither comes nor goes. An event is transient. An experience is simply an observation within time. Reality is not in time, which is why you cannot perceive it.

Be the watcher of events and experiences and you have done all you can do. Do not judge as judgment attempts to make real, which cannot be done. Even science works on theories and postulates. Science knows nothing is absolute.

Life is make-believe. Nothing ever really happens. Whatever appears to happen is just that, an appearance. Once you awaken into reality you will want to stay in reality. The starting point for reality is the silence where nothing enters. Silence is the domain of meditation.

Realize that every mode of perception is subjective. What is seen, heard, touched, smelt, felt, thought, expected or imagined is in the mind and not in reality. Once you get this you will experience peace and freedom from fear. You now have a "place" to go where the world cannot.

Reality is neither subjective nor objective, neither mind nor matter, neither time nor space. These divisions need somebody to whom they happen and there is ultimately no one they can happen to. Reality is all and nothing, the totality and the exclusion, the fullness and the emptiness, fully consistent, absolutely paradoxical.

Advaita –Vedanta

In a literal sense advaita is the teaching of nonduality.

Because most people believe that they live in a state of duality, having eaten from the "tree of knowledge"(the opposites), this teaching is not easy to grasp the first time. The path of unlearning is necessary before one can enter the path of knowledge. That is why Part I is the longest part of this book.

Everything you have been told and learned in duality must be disregarded. The reason is that what you think you know comes from other. The reason it must be disregarded is there is nothing outside you. There is no other.

Ask yourself the following question or series of questions:

Without using my mind, memory, thoughts, emotions, associations or perceptions who am I? Am I a man or a woman or neither? Am I worthy, unworthy or neither? Am I adequate, inadequate or neither? Am I loveable, not loveable or neither? You could put any subject in this exercise.

What did you come up with? I came up with neither.

The true I Am is a no mind state. You cannot verbalize it. It is "neti-neti" (not this, not this). Non-verbal awareness (Non-judgment) is the path to knowing. Forgiveness is waking up. You know for yourself that staying in the no mind state (the Now) creates less confusion and greater happiness. The minute you enter the mind state, disease ensues. You will have to be "out of your mind" to get this. So, strive to stay in the nothing state for as long as it takes to glimpse true awareness. Once you see, you will want to spend more time there.

Becoming a witness to emptiness transcends the verbal state. When there is no frame of reference there can be no reference to frame. Maturity comes in the state of emptiness not in a state of mind chatter. The question is how long can you stay in the silence? Discard all that you are not (your definitions) and go deeper.

Discard all concepts until there is nothing left. Give up the comfort of your definitions. All words and concepts require more words and concepts. There is no original concept to succeed to. It would be better if you had no language to overcome but even this must go.

The outer world is an ever-changing illusion. You designed it that way for your own pleasure. You will never understand the world you made because it is the dominion of the ego. To figure it out would eliminate the ego and that will not happen in apparent reality. The more complicated and fearful you make it the better the ego likes it. Therefore you need the ego to function. Do you get the trick?

There is a world out there but it is not the one you see. There is no competition in absolute reality. There is no conflict, illness, decay or death. These things you must have made up because God certainly didn't make them. You can see the real world but only from the inside-out not the outside-in. Once you see it for what it is you will have a long laugh. When I got it I laughed for hours!

What do you think will happen on December 21, 2012? What difference does it make? Now really, what difference does it make?

By now you should get that if it "matters", it can't be anything but emptiness because matter is empty space filled only with your projections. It will be what you want it to be. It's not about time and space. It's about no time and space. Do you want to be a part of impermanence or do you want to go to home?

For me, I choose heaven.

A NEW WORLD

Some Final Thoughts

Right now your head must be reeling? Good. I can't say I am sorry. My intention was to give you a book to change your life, not entertain you. If you are ready for a serious change, the information in this book must have created an "ah-ha" or two and a "what do I do now question?" The answer is: seek and you will find.

Unless you are out of your comfort zone you will make no adjustments in your life. Unless the planet is threatened it will likewise not respond. Consciousness on this planet will not advance unless it is shaken.

What about you? The urgency to get on with it is either clear at this point or you missed it. This book is about conscious expansion, healing and getting on with it. It's the red pill not the blue.

The stakes are high. We will be entering a new dimension soon. It will be frightening to the unprepared. It's Big Stuff. Are you up for it is the question? Are you sick and tired of being sick and tired? Are you disillusioned with your institutions failure to help you find peace of mind? If your answers are yes then this book is just the beginning.

There is much to do.

What you need to do now is re-read Part II and Part III very slowly. Take some notes. You may want to reread the entire book or get the books I suggested. Then find a teacher or a school.

Part I, The Undoing, gives you permission to get on with it. It is okay to give up on religion. Religion is a defense against God. Religion is the ego's counterfeit version of love. You cannot get on with transformation until you are out of the box. Not partially out but completely out. Religion has put you in a box for 1,500 years. Are you ready to escape or sleep?

Where has religion gotten humanity anyway? Right now we are fighting another religious war on the Asian Continent, which will never end and it could lead to a nuclear exchange. How many need to be killed in the name of some god before we get it? It has never changed since the first Crusade. God has nothing to do with it. That has always been propaganda.

When asked, "what do you really want?" what did you come up with?

Dr. Hawkins suggests that 85% of the world's population is below the 200 conscious level, which means that the vast majority of mankind are asleep. Certainly most people are not ready to receive the information in this book and its references. Very few are ready for transformation and leadership. If you got it that this book is looking for leaders, you got it right. Now is the time to put away childish things and grow up. Are you ready for conscious expansion? It is a one-way street but the ends justify the means. It is not for everyone.

Many are called but few are chosen.

It will take a crisis to get humanities attention. Is that by cataclysm or consciousness shift or both? There are over 6.5 billion souls on spaceship Earth at the present time. Many scientists suggest that the planet's resources are capable of supporting about one-third of that number for the next decade or two at the most. The projections are for 10 billion people by 2030. This space ship just isn't that big! Obviously something has to give.

I do not have a crystal ball but my guess is that planetary changes will become more dramatic in the next three years. We know that solar flares, with incredible coronal mass ejections (CME), will peak in late 2012. Coupled with planetary alignment could bring about the earth changes necessary to reduce world population. You will begin to hear more and more about viruses that are gaining epidemic proportions.

I believe all this is coincidental with the December 21, 2012 prophecies. None of it matters to those who understand that it is not about the body. Regardless of what happens in the illusory physical dimension you cannot die. The body might perish but you are not your body. You are consciousness and consciousness never ends. This is not a time to sit back and take a wait and see attitude. This is a time for action.

The only reality you are interested in is non-dual reality. You have been taught just the opposite. Only non-dual reality is ultimately real. Why invest your energy in illusion? Getting prepared for transformation means being able to handle whatever comes because you understand what is real and what is an illusion. Isn't that comforting?

Only the ignorant are afraid. Strive for enlightenment and the world will disappear.

BIBLIOGRAPHY

The Power of Myth by Joseph Campbell

Don't Know Much About The Bible by Kenneth Davis

Deceptions And Myths Of The Bible by Lloyd M. Graham

Jesus And The Lost Goddess by Timothy Freke and Peter Gandy

The Jesus Mysteries by Timothy Freke and Peter Gandy

The Laughing Jesus by Timothy Freke and Peter Gandy

Lucid Living by Timothy Freke

The Gospel of Judas

The Gospel of Thomas

The Celestine Prophecy and the Celestine Vision by James Redfield

Power vs. Force by David Hawkins

The Power Of Now by Eckhart Tolle

A Course In Miracles (Text, Workbook and Reacher's Manual)

Awakening To Your Call (Exploring A Course in Miracles) by John Mundy

I AM THAT "A Modern Spiritual Classic" Talks with Nisargadatta Maharj